CAREER HEIST

SEIZE CONTROL OF YOUR PROFESSIONAL JOURNEY

APOORV BAMBA
GAURAV GANDHI
LOCHAN NARAYANAN

Published by Westland Business, an imprint of Westland Books, a division of Nasadiya Technologies Private Limited, in 2025

No. 269/2B, First Floor, 'Irai Arul', Vimalraj Street, Nethaji Nagar, Alapakkam Main Road, Maduravoyal, Chennai 600095

Westland, the Westland logo, Westland Business and the Westland Business logo are the trademarks of Nasadiya Technologies Private Limited, or its affiliates.

ISBN: 9789360456269

10 9 8 7 6 5 4 3 2 1

The views and opinions expressed in this work are the authors' own and the facts are as reported by them, and the publisher is in no way liable for the same.

Typeset by Mukul

Printed at Parksons Graphics Pvt. Ltd

CAREER HEIST

Apoorv Bamba is a father who is trying to unlock the mystical world of parenting in the twenty-first century. He also happens to be an entrepreneur often finding himself in a battle with the broken employability system of the country. He loves the art of unlearning and thrives in uncomfortable situations with people and places who challenge his way of being. Lastly, he is a wanderer and loves getting lost in pursuit of constant change and evolution—sometimes for the sake of it!

Gaurav Gandhi is an advisor, mentor and consultant based in Vienna, with nineteen years of global experience at Tata Consultancy Services and Tata Sons. He specialises in helping Austrian and Indian companies collaborate, mentoring start-ups and SMBs, and advising on industry–research partnerships. With expertise spanning IT, innovation and business development, Gaurav has built partnerships with leading academic institutions like Harvard and MIT. A certified international career coach, Ayurvedic Lifestyle Management expert and gold-certified business storyteller, Gaurav is passionate about guiding professionals through meaningful career transitions.

Lochan Narayanan is a Leadership Development professional and ICF (ACC) certified coach with extensive experience across multiple industries. She has worked with organisations such as GE Capital, American Express and ACT Fibernet. As a coach, Lochan works with successful professionals looking for that inflection point in their career that requires them to reevaluate their career and life choices. She has 500+ hours of experience of coaching different professionals navigate career transitions across life stages. She also hosts a podcast called *Career Uninterrupted* focused on building an ecosystem that supports mid-career transitions.

Praise for *Career Heist*

'Imagine going up a mountain and being accompanied by an experienced sherpa to guide you through the terrain. You could have done it yourself, but the sherpa increased your speed, efficiency and certainty. This is a career trek for you. In work and career, with the terrain becoming more and more uncertain and navigating it getting harder, this book couldn't have been more timely.'

—Gurpreet Kalra, Head Talent Development, Tata Consultancy Services (TCS) UK & Ireland

'Gaurav Gandhi was associated with me in TCS for several years. During his tenure in TCS, he navigated complex roles across global teams and industries, which enabled his deep understanding of career transitions and that, coupled with his passion for helping others tackle challenges head-on, makes *Career Heist* a lovely guidebook for thriving in today's ever-evolving work environment. Best wishes to the authors and to the professionals who will benefit now.'

—Dr K. Kesavasamy
Former Software Scientist, ISRO and Former Education Leader, TCS, IEEE Education Society Board of Governors (2025–2027)

'One of the most exciting and scary realities of modern careers is that they are long yet chaotic, rich but non-linear, rewarding but often sharply punctuated by big technology, regulatory and market shifts. In parallel, individual aspirations for what success means are also going through its own churn. Combined, these forces create a unique, unprecedented challenge for early and mid-career professionals: about how to plan, how to execute and how to navigate their careers. This book offers great value in how to approach these dilemmas. It's a must-read for professionals and those who help shape the careers of others, as parents, educators and employers.'

—Shreyasi Singh, Founder,
Harappa Education; ex-President, Capability,
Delivery & Brand, upGrad Enterprise

'This book is doubly pertinent. First, our perspective on career transitions has been limited by the scarcity of experiences that reside in an Indian economic or cultural context. To boot, the handicap magnifies as the Rise of AI reimagines jobs, leading to many more career changes—whether forced or motivated.'

—Amit Bhaskar, Seasoned business executive
with 15+ years in CXO roles globally

'We spend a significant portion of our lives at work, yet the rapidly evolving work environment often demands constant adaptation. This deeply insightful book offers a roadmap for designing a career story that brings meaning not just to work, but to life as a whole. It explores diverse scenarios, from navigating alternative careers to making strategic moves within organisations. Whether the goal is to stay relevant, pivot or embark on an entirely new path, this book equips readers with the tools to thrive in a world of constant change.'

—Raju Goteti, Vice President, Tata Consultancy Services

'Packed with practical tips, real-world insights and relatable questions like, "Why do I feel stuck?" or "Can I start over with a Career 2.0?", this book offers clear answers and actionable advice. Whether you're starting out, reinventing yourself or simply exploring new paths, this guide will help you navigate the twists and turns of your career with confidence.'

—Priyank Narayan, Founding Director, Centre for Entrepreneurship, Ashoka University, bestselling author, *Leapfrog*

Contents

Foreword

THE CONCEPT OF A 'TRADITIONAL CAREER' IS RAPIDLY becoming a thing of the past. The days of working for decades in or retiring from a single company, especially in the private sector, and following a predictable career path, are increasingly rare. In their place, we now find ourselves navigating a world where careers are more purposeful, flexible, fluid, fun and, at times, chaotic.

If you're reading this book, it's likely that you're standing at a crossroads in your own professional journey. Perhaps you're uncertain about where you or your career are headed, or wondering how to make the most from the work you do. You may even be feeling stuck or unfulfilled, or questioning whether there's more to life than just climbing the corporate ladder.

In my experience, a fulfilling career is not just about professional success or climbing the designations ladder. It's about achieving true *life–family–work balance.*

Life: Before diving into your career path, it's crucial to reflect on your personal needs and aspirations—both for yourself and your loved ones. What truly matters to you in life? Is it financial security, family, friendships, health or perhaps contributing to your community? None of us will be able to satisfy all these needs simultaneously, so it's important to prioritise them. Defining your core values and personal goals will give you the clarity you need to shape your career in a way that aligns with your life's vision. This book thoughtfully integrates Maslow's hierarchy of needs and generational diversity, providing valuable frameworks to help guide you in these decisions.

Work: The reality of the modern professional landscape is that what you study and what you actually do will be very different. The half-life of skills (i.e., the time when what you learn becomes obsolete) is shrinking from more than twenty years in the past to five years today with the advent of mobile/Wi-Fi/technology/AI in everything we do at home or at the office.

The currency for future-proofing your career is *skill*—not just a degree, but the ability to adapt, unlearn and continuously learn. In today's world, your experience, mindset and attitude matter far more than your age, degree or grades.

This book is designed as a *101 guide* for early–mid career professionals, offering practical insights, real-world examples and frameworks that will help you rethink and reimagine your career.

In a rapidly changing world, the responsibility for shaping your career is yours to take. I encourage you to use the perspectives in these pages to chart your own course—one that aligns with your values, adapts to new opportunities and positions you for long-term success.

Good luck as you embark on this journey of career discovery and growth. Take charge of your career and shape it in the way that will bring the most fulfilment to you and your family.

Sanjeev Jain
Leader with 30+ years Industry experience across
M&M, HUL, GE, Cognizant, IBM, Wipro

Authors' Note

WRITING A BOOK IS EXTREMELY CHALLENGING! Especially if you have three people trying to co-author the book. The opinions, styles and perspectives vary and sometimes contradict each other as well. We would be lying if we said this was an easy process. However, it was our determination to help mid-level professionals navigate their career that ensured that we stayed on this path.

Each of us have been through this phase and we truly believe that a book like this at that juncture would have really helped us. With this thought in mind, we have written the book in a simple and easy to understand manner, with excerpts from tons of research. We have also interviewed close to a hundred professionals and included their perspectives as well. The stories shared are real examples of people who have made changes and have navigated their careers effectively. While we have changed the names to protect identities, the stories are real!

The book has undergone many versions, with each of us facing writer's block multiple times during the process. We were able to go ahead due to the continued encouragement of our friends and family, who supported us through this entire process. We are especially grateful to Dipti Janardhana, Preeti Ogale, Pallavi Nagarkar, Gurpreet Kalra and Rajeshwari Sharma, for patiently reading the multiple drafts to give us their critical inputs that only encouraged us to make it better.

We are also extremely thankful to Shweta Chaudhary, who worked with us tirelessly to edit the structure of the book and merge the three perspectives into a common thread.

In addition, we are also thankful to the team at Westland Books that decided to support us to bring out a book on this topic.

How should you read this book?

From left to right!

Jokes apart, this book is meant for every mid-level professional who is actively looking to take charge of their career. You can pick up any chapter and read it, and read the book in whichever order you feel most comfortable. You can use this book to draw inspiration from others' stories (there are plenty of them) or understand why you feel restless in your current role or get steps that you can take to work on your career.

The term 'heist' is associated with robbery—we are asking you to steal the reins of your career from someone else and take control of them.

The writers come with varied experiences—from never having worked in a formal corporate set-up to having worked only in one company. Despite these different experiences, our understanding of what helps you steer your career forward falls on a few principles. You may find some principles repeated, but they would have been brought into that section to elaborate that particular context.

Read this book with a bookmark, highlight sections that are relevant to you, keep going back to it. We believe this book can be picked up every few years as some of the exercises given are time agnostic and will hold true even after a few years. More importantly, read this book with an open mind—that allows new perspectives and ideas to enter, along with questioning some beliefs that you may hold about your career.

We really hope you enjoy reading it!

Introduction

It was one of those stormy Mumbai evenings—the kind where time stands still and all you want to do is enjoy the weather from the comfort of your balcony. As you grab a cup of freshly brewed coffee and get comfortable in a chair, the enticing smell of the wet ground envelops you. But as luck would have it, instead of enjoying the breeze on the balcony of my home, I found myself at the airport. To add to my misery, next to my flight's schedule on the board was the dreaded word: DELAYED.

What I have always found interesting about airports—or rather, the airports of today—is that if you take away their core purpose, they are nothing but shopping malls. You can enjoy a range of pricey restaurants and do endless window shopping. Most importantly, you can watch people to your heart's content. But the fact remains that the airport is supposed to be a point in one's transit to the actual destination, which makes one feel uneasy about spending any more time there than is essential.

When I got the disappointing news about my flight being delayed, I chose to do what best I could in that moment—find the nearest lounge. I had just about settled on a couch when I overheard snippets of what sounded like an interesting conversation. Intrigued, I decided to distract myself from my misery by listening to the two people sitting to my left who, I assumed, were colleagues. They talked about career transitions, professional growth and even the deeper meaning of one's work life. I failed at being discreet and was caught trying to listen in on their discussion. To my surprise, they invited me to join them. To my even bigger surprise, I learnt that both of them had just met at the airport lounge. Theirs, too, was a 'delayed flight connection'!

We spent the next ninety minutes talking about a range of things—from career coaching to therapy and empathy mapping. The three of us had had different career paths and came with our own baggage and biases. However, we realised, despite the differences in our experiences, there were many overlaps. I, Apoorv, have worked mostly with start-ups. Gaurav has been loyal to one big corporation but has explored different roles and even switched between departments. Lochan has tasted both sides of the working world, starting out with sales, then moving to the HR function without any formal degree, and eventually becoming an entrepreneur.

What if we could come together to challenge career wisdom, we wondered. We could share real stories and give access to the tools that have guided us in our professional journeys. And that is how the crazy idea of co-authoring *Career Heist* was born.

What we aim to do through this book on careers is—to draw an analogy—provide you with ingredients to cook your favourite dish. We also want to give you a taste of the possible outcomes based on the recipe you choose.

When it comes to work, our current reality is beyond what we could have imagined even a decade ago. COVID-19 has shaped us in ways we never expected. Whether it is for the better or worse, the pandemic has changed many things about doing business and also about the way we work. Not everything has settled in yet; some aspects are still finding their adjusted identity in the new normal. We have seen the evolution of employability, employment and the future of work up close. Ever since the pandemic changed our lives in unprecedented and unpredictable ways, we've been front-row passengers on the career heist roller coaster. We faced resistance to remote work. We also faced challenges in getting people back to work. We experienced the great resignation and saw employees move between companies in the same sector. We've also seen early retirements and the reverse migration of professional talent. We've seen unheard-of 'breaking the ceiling' salary packages and mass firings.

The best way to describe this book would be to compare it to a road trip which has a destination called 'Career'. It prepares you for the journey of a lifetime and equips you with practical tips and tricks to navigate through diverse—and sometimes difficult—terrains. We, the authors, are a bunch of cheerleaders who are eager to provide guidance on this journey. We will help you make the following decisions and navigate some interesting questions:

- Why do I feel stuck in my career? Is it okay to feel so?
- What is the future of work? How can I prepare myself for the same?
- Is there a perfect role for me? How do I find it?
- Can I build my career in the same company? Does that still make me 'cool'?
- Can I have a Career 2.0?
- What do I need to navigate through this maze called 'career'?

Career Heist is the road map to consult for the best way to get to destination 'Career'.

chapter one

Are You Feeling Stuck?

JUNE 2014. IT WAS A WARM DAY AND GAURAV HAD BOARDED a bus from his home in Chembur for his office in Andheri, a suburb of Mumbai. He had been working with a leading IT services company for ten years. He had earlier been part of two long assignments, stationed in Germany and Canada. Now, Gaurav had a team of thirty-five people across nine locations around the world. He was working on an excellent project. Additionally, he was contributing to market communications for the account and was responsible for leading process improvement.

Even though others thought he had a good job, a feeling of discomfort had been gnawing at him for the last few weeks. When he reached the office that day, he suddenly realised what was bothering him. The thought that he may end up being on the same career path for the next decade of his life suddenly made him feel like he was stuck.

An average person spends 90,000 hours of their life at work. It's not surprising to feel stuck in one's career at some point in time. Many people feel regret and self-doubt about their careers. According to a survey of a thousand people conducted by Zety.com,[1] the most common top career regrets of people were:

1. Not taking more initiative
2. Not having enough mentorship or guidance
3. Playing it safe or not taking more chances
4. Not growing their network
5. Not quitting a job they disliked sooner
6. Not negotiating hard enough for raises
7. Not focusing enough on advancing their career
8. Not maintaining their network
9. Not negotiating a higher starting salary
10. Not working harder in school

You may be able to relate to one or more of these regrets. It happens to all of us. Most of these regrets happen when we are stuck in a role that no longer lives up to our expectations. But it's tough to leave that role as one may have fallen into one of the five traps:[2]

1. *Ambition trap*: High achievers fear that slowing down will hinder their success. When they face pressure at work, they work even harder. However, they find it challenging to relax and take a break.

2. *Expectation trap*: Some people always try to meet the expectations of others. They may find it hard to recognise when they are overworked or burnt out. They fear that admitting these struggles could harm their reputation or ego.
3. *Busyness trap*: People who fall into this trap feel fulfilled by being busy all the time and putting work first. As a result, they may have a hard time saying no or taking breaks, which results in them neglecting their health and relationships.
4. *Translation trap*: Even successful people can be affected by this. Those caught in this trap may feel unsatisfied and disconnected from their purpose, even though they have accomplished a lot. They may also worry that changing direction would mean giving up all their hard work.
5. *Adrenaline trap*: Many people begin to rely on adrenaline to keep them going. They forget to take care of themselves and take breaks. Yet, it's important to remember that self-care is necessary for a long-lasting career and effective leadership.

As you navigate your career journey, it's easy to fall into these traps without even realising it. Take the case of Sarah, for instance. A marketing manager with ten years of experience, she excelled in her role, consistently exceeding targets and climbing up the corporate ladder. However, she started feeling a nagging dissatisfaction despite her achievements. At first, she brushed it off, thinking it was just a phase. But as the weeks turned into months, Sarah found herself working late into the night, sacrificing her weekends, and feeling increasingly disconnected from her purpose. She realised she was caught in the ambition trap and the busyness trap, always pushing harder without taking a moment to breathe.

Her story isn't unique; many mid-career professionals find themselves in similar situations, trapped by the very roles that once brought them joy and fulfilment. If Sarah's experience resonates with you, it's time to take a step back and assess your current role. The following exercise will guide you through a reflective process to help you identify these traps and take actionable steps towards a more satisfying career.

Exercise 1: Assess Your Current Role

This is an indicative exercise that can help you assess your current role. There are enough distractions in the environment that can make you restless. Answering these questions will help you understand if you need to take action that will change the course of your career, or if you simply need to stop scrolling through social media!

S. No.	Question	Most of the time/ Sometimes/Never
1	Do I like my work?	
2	Do I like working with my manager?	
3	Do I like working with my peers?	
4	Does the role allow me to explore new avenues?	
5	Do I get to learn in the role?	
6	Does the role pay me enough?	
7	Does the role give me stress?	
8	Do I get treated respectfully at work?	
9	Do I get feedback about my work periodically?	

S. No.	Question	Most of the time/ Sometimes/Never
10	Does the role provide a certain stability to my life?	
11	Does the role have enough elements of change and variety?	
12	Do I get a sense of purpose by working in this organisation?	
13	Do I like working with my current clients/ stakeholders?	

- If the responses to at least ten questions are 'Most of the time'/'Sometimes', then you need to understand your reason for restlessness in your role better.
- If the responses to at least ten questions are 'Sometimes'/'Never', you may want to explore roles that allow you to answer all of these questions positively.

How to View Your Career?

When a person feels a sense of stagnation, they often think of quitting their job. Many do something similar when triggered by an incident or a series of events, which may include delayed promotions, poor appraisals, unclear responsibilities and so on. When something about your current job triggers you, you feel quitting your job is the solution to your problems. But this is rarely how things work. You may run away from your current problems but will most likely land into even bigger ones. When you are dissatisfied with any aspect of your current job, the offer of a new job and the benefits associated with it look more tempting than they are. You consider the potential positive outcomes of the new job. As you do so, you overlook the various problems that could arise in your new job, which may be even worse than those in your current job. In essence, you suffer from the 'outcome bias'.

As professionals, we all get tempted by the lure of a better career. Sometimes, this is triggered by the success of others, sometimes by our own lack of progress, and sometimes by the sheer sense of sameness and boredom in our current role.

You may be actively or passively browsing a new role. But before you decide to quit, identify how you view your career.

Approach Your Career Like a Game

Has your approach to your career ever reminded you of any game? There are some interesting insights on drawing such a comparison.[3] Some of the common games that people play to succeed in their careers are:

- *Climb the ladder*: Here, one follows the traditional promotion path, step by step.
- *Follow the leader*: It's self-explanatory—do what the boss says!
- *Follow your heart*: Pursue your dreams.
- *Commit 100 per cent*: This involves working as hard as you can.
- *Make a living*: In this, you think of your job as a paycheque to support your passion, lifestyle or family.
- *Shine the brightest*: For this, you need to find something no one else has done before—and do it.
- *Don't rock the boat*: Go along with the group and be a good team player.
- *Outlast your rivals*: Keep going until everyone else gives up.
- *Play not to lose*: Avoid risk to ensure that your career survives.
- *Play to win*: The belief guiding this approach is: No guts, no glory. Who cares about second place?

- *Do whatever it takes*: Here, you must be creative—and beware of compromising your ethics.

You would have certainly identified a few games from this list that you may have played unintentionally throughout your career. It's crucial to take a moment to evaluate which career games you're currently engaged in.

Are you playing a game that aligns with your values and abilities, or are you merely comfortable with it? For instance, you may have started out with 'Climb the ladder' but given your current life stage and ambition, you may no longer align with it. You may feel that continuing to climb the ladder will lead to a dead end very soon and so you may now want to change the game.

It's important to play a game that genuinely inspires you. If you feel bored, stressed, unfulfilled or empty, it may be time to consider switching to a new game. It's perfectly acceptable to change your game many times until you find one that is gratifying and motivating for you.

There's one challenge though. Usually, our workstyles and habits are shaped by the game we started with. Thus, changing the game—even if we understand the need for a change—may not be as easy. In such a case, you may want to evaluate if a career break or a job change will enable you to reset your mindset.

Will a Career Break Help You Feel Unstuck?

Do you really need another role or will a break solve the problem? There are many reasons why people take career breaks. Some of the common ones include maternity leave or spending time with young children, relocating for a spouse struggling to find a new job, caring for sick parents, taking a study break, experiencing burnout, or just needing time to think about the future. In India, taking a career break is now more acceptable than it was a few decades ago. This is because the country is getting wealthier, which leads to more choices, so taking breaks is feasible. The biggest aspect of taking a break is the accompanying financial burden, but with proper planning, this is possible. Both start-ups and corporates have started being more open to the idea of a career break. Corporates have started to value an entrepreneurial or a start-up stint and consider them as legitimate work experiences, which was not the case a few decades ago.

When you're thinking about your career and trying to figure out what you need—a transition, a break or a move to a different company—here are some factors you can consider.

1. **Are you being paid fairly?**

- Look at websites like Glassdoor and AmbitionBox to compare your salary with those in similar roles and with similar experience.

- Try to get some competing offers from the market to check where you stand.
- Check with a friend who applied for a parallel job in your company and find the difference. If it is large (let's say more than 50 per cent) then it may indicate that you are not being paid as per market standards.

2. **Does your employer offer flexible working arrangements?**

- Discuss flexible working arrangements with your manager. This is especially important for working couples with young kids or ageing parents.

3. **Does your organisation have clear career paths and growth opportunities?**

- Check for a clear career path outlining the next roles and skills required for it.
- Look for internal job posting options in your company that allow you to move across roles.
- Look for examples of people who have moved ahead in defined career paths.

4. **Does your organisation provide clear learning opportunities?**

- Check for learning opportunities to ensure that you stay relevant and can grow in your career. Does your organisation actively support your training?

- Discuss with your manager if you can be put in cross-functional projects.

A career break would be an ideal step in the following scenarios:

- You are aligned with the overall organisation values but want to try another role which the organisation cannot offer.
- You want to rethink your current career trajectory and have the financial security to quit.
- You want to move to another country with your spouse but don't have a job offer.
- You are feeling a certain level of burnout and want to rethink the next steps in your career.
- You want to move to a city of choice (for family or personal reasons) and want to look for opportunities in those cities.

While a career break allows you to pause and reflect, it is also prudent to plan your finances to support the same.

Will a Job Change Solve Your Problem?

Sometimes, your role is not the problem, the job is. We have an interesting example of this. In the early 2000s, Parag completed his studies in mechanical engineering and joined a government research institute. However, he soon realised that government organisations paid low salaries and had few future growth opportunities. So, he changed direction and joined the thriving IT sector. He became a simulation engineer for a large automotive customer at one of India's leading IT services companies. Within a year and a half of joining the organisation, he moved to the US, thereby gaining international exposure. In Parag's case, changing his job was all he needed to dispel the constant feeling of being stuck that had been gnawing at him. What Parag seems to have done was to change his game from 'Climb the ladder' to 'Make a living'. As long as one's game is aligned to what one aspires to achieve at any given stage, it enables them to do well.

While 'Make a living' may seem like Parag was only focused on salary or a higher monetary gain, we need to remember that jobs are not only means of getting a paycheque at the end of the day. In fact, each job pays you five salaries:[4]

- *Financial:* Annual salary, bonuses, equity, healthcare, benefits, etc.
- *Psychological:* The internal and external meaning you derive from your work. Your connection to the mission, the product, the work you produce and the praise you receive.
- *Social:* Prestige, job title and the identity capital you receive.

- *Education:* Skills, relationships and learnings that contribute to your development as a person and professional.
- *Freedom:* Your ability to work on your terms.

When we're unhappy at work, we often focus on getting more of the wrong 'salary'. For example, negotiating a raise ('financial') when the problem is psychological. Gopal's story will explain the concept better.

Gopal had over ten years of experience in the IT field and was doing well. However, he was not very happy with his work in the current role, as it was monotonous. He felt a change in role would excite him and so, he set up a meeting with his HR partner, Ritika, to discuss any alternate roles for him. During these discussions, Gopal informed Ritika that his spouse was a working professional and they were parents to two young kids. He was doing well in financial, social and educational aspects. He thought the issue was psychological and a role change was the solution.

Ritika gave him this advice: 'Take your career decisions based on what stage of life you are in.' At the stage he was in, he needed stability, and a role change, while providing challenges, might leave him with less time with his family. She recommended that he continue in his current role and discuss with his manager how to get more challenging work to utilise his experience and expertise. This flexible arrangement would ensure the required stability while he also learnt new skills.

Gopal's situation is not unique. Many professionals, especially those in mid-career, find themselves in similar predicaments. It is important that we constantly evaluate the priority order of these salaries along with what our role offers for each of them. The priority order may change at different life stages. It's crucial to recognise when a job no longer fulfils the essential 'salaries' necessary for your well-being and career growth. Ignoring these signals can lead to deeper dissatisfaction and burnout.

Is It Time to Quit Your Job?

What if you find you are not getting all the required salaries from your job? How should you decide if it is time to leave your job? There are six warning signs[5] that give you a hint, and it is important to evaluate the situation objectively.

1. *It's no longer encouraging your growth.*
   The job is no longer helping you grow. In fact, it is hindering your growth. You feel stagnated and see no options but to rediscover yourself.

2. *You've achieved what you set out to achieve.*
   You've achieved your purpose with the job, and it's not motivating enough to show up every day. Apoorv was interviewing someone for a mid-level role at his organisation. He asked her about the organisation she was in and why she was looking for

a change. Her response was: 'I have been with them for three years, and I have got everything I could out of this role. I spoke to my Founder and requested a role change, but it was not possible for them. Now, I am seeking a new opportunity to further diversify my career trajectory.' The candidate's response was valid. Even if the role is outstanding, you can still outgrow it after two to three years.

3. *You actively look for ways to avoid your job.*
   You procrastinate going to work, and Sunday scares have become the new normal for you.

4. *You regularly approach work with exhaustion, burnout or dread.*
   You feel tired just looking at the to-do list. You are exhausted by the thought of the work itself.

5. *It's causing you to develop bad habits.*
   You've started developing unhealthy habits as revenge procrastination. Your smoke breaks have increased, or you have been binge-eating and binge-watching to escape work stress.

6. *Your workplace has become unhealthy.*
   Your workplace has become toxic. Common signs are a lack of work–life balance, unhealthy competition and intrusive management. You can see its negative effects on your physical health or mental health.

If these six signs look familiar, then you certainly need to change something. Whether it's a job change or an entire career transition, you will figure it out as you move forward with the book.

How to Get the Right Support for Your Career Progression

What if taking a break or changing your job is not the solution? What if you need to figure out your career all over again? It is overwhelming to rethink your entire progression alone. You are not sure which role will suit your skills, and whether there is a good market or employment opportunities for the skills you have. And how do you make that first move? Everything feels scary. The good news is you don't have to figure out everything on your own. You can always get the right support by (1) seeking feedback and (2) finding mentors. Let's walk you through how you can do this.

How to Get Honest Feedback

'Feedback is a free education to excellence. Seek it with sincerity and receive it with grace.'

—Ann Marie Houghtailing

What you need is genuine feedback, but it's usually hard to get honest feedback as people tend to be politically correct. Sometimes, you have to ask them in a way that shows you're comfortable with receiving honest feedback. In the exercise that follows, we have templatised the entire process for you. Once you receive feedback, it is up to you to act on it and show progress. This always encourages the feedback giver to share more inputs in your journey.

Exercise 2: Getting 360-degree Feedback for Yourself

Feedback that is sought from an individual's subordinates, peers, colleagues and supervisor, and also includes a self-evaluation, is called a 360-degree feedback. Organisations usually do a 360-degree assessment for employees to identify their development needs and growth potential. Such a feedback process is usually managed and administered by external partners.

As individuals, we can use the principles of 360-degree feedback and get some insights into our own development plan. You can hire a formal organisation to do this for you in a structured manner. This will have a cost implication.

In case you would like to do this in a simpler manner, you can use the structure shared here. In this exercise, be mindful that the people giving you feedback are concerned about your well-being and therefore the responses may be more positively skewed than you like.

However, this is a great starting point to get an idea of how you are being perceived and what you can do differently going forward.

Step 1: Make a list of people you would like to get feedback from.

This could include: managers and former managers; team members, those reporting to you as well as those who formerly reported to you; peers; stakeholders and internal clients as well as anyone else whose views you trust. You can list them down in a simple grid like the one below.

Managers/ Former managers	Team members/ Reportees	Peers	Stakeholders/ Clients

Step 2: Reach out for feedback.

Reach out to each of these individuals with a request to share feedback about you and your work. You can use the following template for your email or message.

Hi ___________

Hope you are doing well.

I am creating my own development plan and looking to get feedback from different people for the same.

We had worked together on/in ______________ and I am sure during this period there would have been things that you may have observed about me and my work style.

I will share with you a form/set of questions that has some areas that I would like to get feedback on.

I would appreciate honest and candid feedback from you. This will not be shared anywhere and will be used only for me to improve myself.

Thank you

Regards

____

Step 3: Seek feedback in a structured way.

You can decide the themes that you would like to explore and create a set of questions accordingly. You can use any format—a simple WhatsApp message, an email, a Google form or any other format that you are comfortable with. The questions broadly remain the same across the groups.

Here's an indicative list, which you can build upon and customise for your feedback needs.

Questions	Managers	Peers	Team	Others
According to you, what are my three key strengths? Can you elaborate by providing actual examples/ instances?				
What are my three areas of improvement? Can you elaborate by providing examples/ instances?				
What are some strengths that you feel I am not utilising fully?				

Questions	Managers	Peers	Team	Others
What are my top three leadership strengths? Can you provide examples/ instances for these?				
How well do I work under pressure?				
How well do I work with other people?				
How well do I lead my teams?				
How well do I manage difficult conversations?				

Step 4: Collate the results to arrive at themes and trends.

Receiving honest feedback can be challenging, but it's a critical part of career progression. Once you've gathered the feedback, take some time to reflect on it objectively. Here are some steps to handle the feedback effectively:

1. *Acknowledge and thank*: Start by thanking everyone who provided feedback. A simple message of appreciation shows that you value their input and encourages them to continue being honest with you in the future.
2. *Identify key themes*: Look for recurring themes or comments in the feedback you've received. For example, if multiple people mention that you need to improve your time management skills, this is a clear area to focus on.
3. *Create an action plan*: Develop a plan to address the feedback. If the feedback indicates a need for better communication skills, you might consider enrolling in a communication workshop or seeking out resources to help improve in this area.
4. *Seek clarification*: If certain feedback is unclear, don't hesitate to reach out for more details. For instance, if a peer mentions that you need to be more collaborative but doesn't provide specifics, ask them to elaborate with examples so you can understand better.
5. *Monitor progress*: Set measurable goals based on the feedback and regularly check your progress. Share your improvements with those who provided the feedback. For example, if you were advised to enhance your leadership skills, keep track of your progress and discuss it with your mentor or supervisor.

6. *Stay positive and open*: Accept feedback with a positive attitude. View it as an opportunity for growth rather than criticism.

Remember, the purpose of this exercise is to not only identify areas for improvement but also recognise and build upon your strengths. Embrace the process, stay open to continuous learning, and you'll find yourself on a clear path to career progression.

How to Find the Right Mentor

After the first couple of years of working, we forget all about being mentored. We feel it is someone else's job to take us under their wings and mentor us. Mentoring is an active relationship. A mentor can guide you professionally and personally in your career. They can enable the best in you with periodic feedback. Having a mentor who has already achieved what you aspire to can be very helpful. For example, F.C. Kohli was the first CEO of TCS. He is known as the father of the Indian IT industry. He mentored S. Ramadorai, the second CEO of TCS. Similarly, Ramadorai mentored N. Chandrasekaran, the next CEO of TCS. N. Chandrasekaran is now the chairman of Tata Sons. He mentored Rajesh Gopinathan, who took over as CEO from him.

You can figure out your ideal career progression with the help of a mentor. They can guide you and give insights into the challenges you may face and the best path to take. Indeed, examining successful careers reveals that many involve mentor–mentee relationships.

When it comes to mentorship, don't focus only on top executives or famous individuals. Many people make this mistake. However, celebrities or very senior professionals often have many people seeking their attention and may not have time to assist a stranger. Instead, focus your efforts on connecting with individuals who are slightly ahead of you. Not only are these people likely to have the bandwidth to assist you, but they will also be able to share more relevant and contextual advice. For instance, try to find and connect with someone who has recently made a similar career change as you and is at the same seniority level. They are more likely to provide helpful advice and assistance.

Here are some steps on how to build an effective mentor–mentee relationship[6]:

- Finding mentors involves considering your self-interest as a driving force. To find out why a potential mentor would want to help you, figure out what you can offer in return. For example, you can help them with their social media, video editing or marketing if they need it.
- Successful people are often busy, so it's best to avoid sending long emails or asking questions that are hard to answer. Demonstrate that you value their time by making concise and straightforward requests.
- To establish a mentor–mentee relationship, you don't just declare yourself as someone's mentee. It's better to see a potential mentor as someone you can ask for advice sometimes. When you get advice from someone you respect, it's important to use it and tell them what happened. By showing that you're committed and willing to take action, you increase the chances of getting more help from them later.
- Don't assume that just adding someone as a connection on LinkedIn will make them want to

be your mentor. Instead, try sending a personalised message through LinkedIn or email. Help them with a project they're working on and try to add value to the situation.

How to find the right mentor:

- Start by identifying individuals who possess the skills, knowledge and experience you aspire to have. For example, if you want to do a career transition within your own organisation, say from software development to marketing, then someone who has travelled that path would be the best fit for you.
- Look within your own network, industry associations or professional groups for potential mentors. LinkedIn can be a great place to begin.
- Many organisations run an internal mentoring programme, which has a large pool of trained and interested mentors. Check if your organisation has such an initiative, and sign up.
- Explore external platforms like Topmate, which list thousands of mentors. Based on their requirements and credentials, you can select the right fit for you.
- Reach out to the individuals you shortlist with a clear and concise message expressing your admiration for their work and your interest in learning from them.

- Start with a discovery call or, if possible, a coffee meeting of half an hour, where you can check if you have the right fit.
- When approaching potential mentors, demonstrate your commitment to personal and professional growth and be specific about what you hope to gain from the mentorship.

But what if you are not able to find a mentor?

Engaging A Career Coach for Transition

Another great way to seek support to navigate a career transition is to work with a career coach. A career coach can help you choose a career, find professional development opportunities and support you in your job search. Hiring a career coach can be very useful in many situations; for instance, if you're not sure about your next career step, need help making a strong and short resume, haven't been successful in job interviews or are having trouble moving forward in your current career.

Career coaches are not the same as career counsellors.

Career counsellors work with students. They review a student's grades, profile and test scores. They then recommend courses or colleges the student can apply to. They also help the students apply to these colleges.

Career coaches don't have expertise in the list of jobs that are out there nor do they help you get that job.

Instead, they work with you at a certain career stage where you feel stuck or confused. They help you think clearly, create career goals, develop action plans and act as your accountability partner. Career coaching is more nuanced and works with individuals on their mindset, attitude and sometimes specific skills.

LinkedIn is a good starting point to find the right career coach who fits your needs. You can also reach out to your friend circle for suggestions. A short discovery call at the start would help you find the fitment with a career coach.

Key Takeaways

- Approach your career like a game. It's perfectly acceptable to change your game many times until you find one that is gratifying and motivating.
- Sometimes a break is the right answer, and sometimes, a job change. Find what's right for you.
- It is overwhelming to rethink your entire progression and plan a transition alone. The good news is you don't have to figure out everything on your own. You can always get the right support by seeking feedback and finding mentors.

chapter two

Is It Too Late to Change Your Career?

'I AM TOO OLD FOR THIS!' ANITHA KEPT SAYING THIS repeatedly while shaking her head.

This was her third coaching session with Lochan. Anitha had come to her as she was feeling stuck in her work. Through the course of the sessions, she had the realisation that she needed to rethink her career. She wanted to feel unstuck, but it was something that was impossible for her (or so she felt).

Anitha was a forty-eight-year-old media ad salesperson who had built her career in the same industry over the last twenty-four years. She had worked in many geographies and had done different types of media ad sales. She had been working in a large global media company for over seven years now. Of late, she had started to notice a significant shift in the company's priorities. They were moving more to online media platforms—OTT, online publications and so on.

The reality of the online media world was different from hers. Though she was meeting her target month on month, she had been feeling she had reached a dead end. Offline media ad sales were decreasing. The market had become saturated.

Anitha was discussing this with a colleague who suggested that she work with a coach to address her feeling of being stuck in her role. That's how Anitha came to have this conversation with Lochan.

Anitha is not the only one to feel this way. In her case, it was evident that technological shifts were making her feel redundant. Most people feel stuck in their careers at some point, even if technological shifts don't directly affect them. This usually happens during mid-career. At such a juncture, people often ask themselves if this is how they had envisaged their career. Some find themselves at the cusp of growth, others get a bitter taste of reality. Some like Anitha end up feeling irrelevant and redundant.

We need to change the lens with which we view careers. Careers no longer look like ladders, and the term 'corporate ladder' is likely to become outdated very soon. Today, careers look more like rock climbing walls with multiple peaks being climbed one after the other. Each mountain has a different terrain, a different route and requires different strengths.

Non-linear Career Path vs Job Hopping

There was a time when a career meant picking a lane and staying on it throughout your working life. But increasingly, career paths are becoming non-linear. A non-linear career path is different from job hopping, which involves frequently changing jobs to get higher pay and job status. Employers often see job hoppers as unreliable, unless they have valid reasons for their moves. On the other hand, a non-linear career path is deliberate and necessitates some level of foresight and strategy.

We hear all these different perspectives, yet we feel our career is going to be uninterrupted. We hold on to the old school of thought—that we'd work in the same career till we are sixty, then retire and enjoy the rest of our life.

COVID-19 taught us that work and how we work can get disrupted overnight. It led us to arrive at a new normal where remote work has gained much greater acceptance and non-linear career paths have become more prevalent.

This new approach to work is likely to become an integral part of our future. Let's get some macro perspectives to understand why this will be the case.

- The rate of technological disruption has increased, giving rise to new industries every few years.[1,2]
- There is geopolitical instability, which is causing constant disruption to how we work.

- Psychological shift—moving up Maslow's hierarchy
- Change in societal constructs

The rise of new industries

In Anitha's case, technological disruption made her successful career feel redundant.

Every few years, we see new technological disruption that gives rise to new full-fledged industries while putting traditional industries at risk. Such technological disruptions call for new sets of skills to run the newly emerging sectors.

It wouldn't be incorrect to say that some skills have not even been identified yet, especially in the world of technology. We need to be aware of what new trends are around the corner and how each is going to disrupt our current way of working. While we need not be wary of these disruptions, we need to be aware of how to incorporate them in our current way of working.

A great example here is of ChatGPT and how it has disrupted the way students write their exams or their essays or even theses. ChatGPT feels scary because it can disrupt many jobs. However, it's important to realise that it's not about man vs machine. It's really about people who can work with machines. A new job that has started to emerge is that of a ChatGPT prompt engineer[3] who can provide the right prompts to ChatGPT to come up with relevant responses or solutions.

Who knew giving prompts could also be an employable skill!

Geopolitical instability

The last few years have shown us the depths of connectedness in the world. The two major geopolitical issues—COVID-19 and the Russia–Ukraine war—have created a new imbalance. Both these incidents have changed the course of work for a lot of industries and organisations, many of which have begun exploring remote work for their employees. When organisations operating in a relatively stable environment like Europe suddenly found themselves in the middle of a war, it changed their internal dynamics.

While in some ways, the war is realigning the world order with India trying to play a critical role, the levels of uncertainty have increased for individuals. We are today living in a BANI world:[4]

B—Brittle

A—Anxious

N—Non-linear

I—Incomprehensible

We all found ourselves at our wits' end when the way we work, our workspaces and how we look at our work life broke down due to the pandemic. It left us anxious and nervous, with a sense of fragility.

The last couple of years have shown people how vulnerable they are—losing loved ones suddenly, losing their jobs overnight, losing their homes forever. This has been a cause of anxiety for people, who have realised that stability and certainty are not assured.

This anxiety is affecting how we all view work. We want a better work–life balance. We also want improved work relationships. Most importantly, we want purpose and meaning in our lives. Of course, this creates its own set of challenges. The current structure of roles and opportunities may not help a person explore this at length.

Psychological shifts

The American psychologist Abraham Harold Maslow came up with the theory of a five-tier model of human needs. Maslow's prepotent hierarchy is based on fulfilling human needs in the order of priority: physiological, safety, social, esteem and self-actualisation.

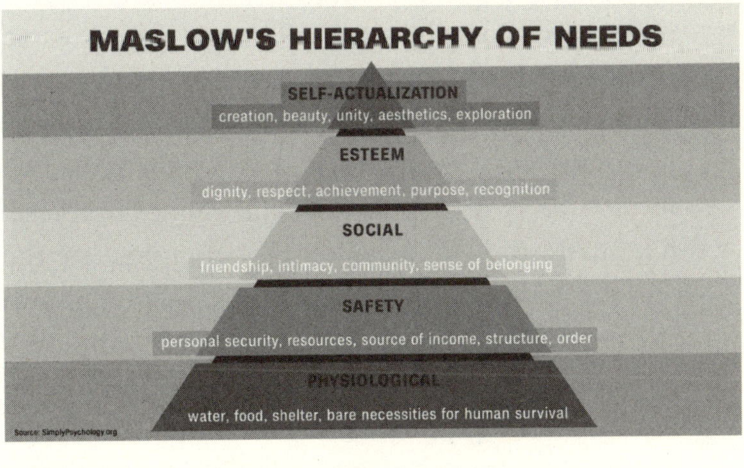

While Maslow set down the hierarchy of needs for individuals, there is also a collective interpretation of this. Where we are as a society helps us decide what kind of things we value the most in our environment. This is applicable to collective selves—family, workplace, neighbourhood, cities, countries, etc.

In India, there has been a shift in this hierarchy of needs.

- Until the late 1980s, most working professionals focused on the basic needs of food, water, safety and security. In fact, work was not supposed to be pleasurable. It was something that was done in order to earn everyday living and support the requirements of the future. The baby boomers (people born between 1946 and 1964) and the early Gen X (people born between 1964 and 1980) fell in this category. Work on weekdays was supposed to provide for the weekends and thus it was expected to be boring and unexciting and a lot of hard work.
- Millennials (born between 1980 and 1996) came in with security from the previous generation. Their parents had already taken care of the basic requirements, which meant they could focus on the next level of requirements at their workplace. Millennials wanted a sense of belonging so the concepts of workplace culture and belongingness started gaining importance. E-sat (employee satisfaction) surveys started to play a critical role in their decision to choose an organisation.

- The latest generation to join the workforce is Gen Z (people born between 1997 and 2012), who have grown up with the internet. They have been exposed to the world from a very young age and a sense of belonging comes naturally to them. Therefore, they collectively look at esteem and a sense of purpose as their primary drivers at the workplace.

As a mid-career professional, you will find similarities with Gen Z. You have surpassed basic needs, which creates a desire to fulfil higher needs. 'But what's the point of doing this? What purpose does it serve?' You may find yourself asking this question again and again. In the process, you may find yourself questioning the way you work.

Change in social constructs

While continuing to be a largely conservative and patriarchal country, we are seeing a shift in the social constructs around us. More people are choosing to marry late or getting divorced or not marrying at all. More and more people are having children late or not having them at all. This shift in the social construct has also led to life and lifestyle changes, with individuals, families and society at large moving away from traditional structures. The shift in the social construct is even influencing career choices, with people now looking at their careers from a non-traditional perspective.

The new realities and the changing perspective about why and how we work pose challenges. However, they also present an opportunity to rewrite our career narrative. It requires an entire mindset shift for us to look at what we have achieved so far without feeling it defines what we can achieve in the future. The mindset shift should enable us to think we can always change directions mid-career too and create a new identity for ourselves.

So how do we change our outlook towards our career and ourselves?

We need to relook at some of the paradigms or principles that we have been operating with. They are not easy. They go down to our beliefs and personalities and thus may require a little effort.

Research has shown that burnout happens when there is a clash between what one 'should be doing' and what 'one will naturally do'. Thus, if we are feeling a sense of burnout or lack of direction, we need to take a deeper look at our beliefs to see if they are still favouring us.

As Marshall Goldsmith said, 'What got you here, won't get you there.'

Four Paradigms of a Transition Process

Based on her experience with different clients, Lochan shares four paradigms that one needs to rethink during a transition process.

1. Define your version of 'success'

We have interviewed over a hundred individuals who have undergone various career transitions. We found one common thread among them. They defined their version of success and kept updating these versions periodically.

Jaspreet, a marketing professional in a large multinational company, felt that her definition of success lay in her ability to control her own time. She took different career paths but finally ended up becoming a wellness coach in a city where she breathes clean air and her kids can walk to school. This was her version of success and she opted for it.

Technology and industry have changed. Now, there are many ways to meet your financial needs and pursue your dreams. This can help you achieve success on your own terms.

Success can mean different things to different people: for some, it could mean a different title, for others more money and for yet others it may mean more free time to pursue their areas of interest outside their work or the ability to work in an area that they are truly passionate about.

The first question YOU need to ask yourself is: 'What does success look like to me?' Success doesn't mean the same thing for everyone. Moreover, it doesn't even have to be the same thing for an individual as it was ten years ago. Our definitions of success as an individual can also change with time. With each decade, there is a change in our life stage and social constructs, and these too contribute to how we define success for ourselves at any point in our life. It is important to keep checking in to see if the definition you created a decade ago holds true even now.

2. We are going to have at least two or three careers in our lifetime.

The first shift we need to make is to accept that we will have at least two or three careers in our lifetime, with each lasting about a decade or so. This means we need to break down our overall career into chunks of a decade each.

The average lifespan of Indians has gone up from around sixty-two in 1999 to seventy-one in 2023—all within a span of twenty-five years.[5] This number is improving year on year, and soon our average lifespan is going to be upwards of eighty years with an active life till the age of seventy. If you start working at the age of twenty-two, careers will need to last or at least financially support you till you are seventy. For ease, let's make it seventy-two. Therefore, you will have a fifty-year period of work life to consider.

When we say career, we don't necessarily mean a 9–6 job. It could be flexible, part-time, but it must have a financial reward and a visible purpose.

Our retired lives will not be like the ones of our parents' generation. We may have more control over our time, but we will need to be physically, mentally and financially active.

We need to divide this fifty-year period into at least three periods of fifteen years each, which means we need to consider where we are in our career every ten years or so. At these junctures, we need to think of the direction we want to take.

The first step in rethinking our career is to recognise this facet and accept it clearly.

If you have spent ten years in a particular career, enjoying the role, the title and the job, it is time for you to rethink the next steps in your career. It is easier to do this when there is no urgency to do so. Urgency, like a job loss or burnout, may force a career shift or change, but a career shift is best done in a conscious way with a deliberate thought process backing it. Ask yourself questions like:

- What do I want the next decade to look like?
- What kind of work do I want to do?
- What kind of people do I want to work with?
- What kind of environment do I want to be in?

The next step is to identify relevant skills, recent market trends and related opportunities. (Refer to this exercise in the previous chapter.)

3. Your career is not your identity.

In a coaching session with Lochan, a senior leader said, 'I don't know what I am in the absence of a career. For the last two decades, my identity, self-worth and pride have come from my career. In the absence of the same, I don't know how to look at myself!'

The person was a casualty of the mass layoffs that happened in some large tech companies.

For most of us, our self-worth is very closely linked to our career. If we have a certain title, responsibilities, salary or perks, our career is going well. It means we are worth something. In the absence of a well-defined career, we are not sure of our value and contribution to the world.

In today's world, careers are fragile. They can no longer define how we add value and what we contribute to the world or people around us.

Lochan helped this client to see his self-worth in other areas of his life using the Value Wheel (Exercise 3). She also helped him understand how he contributed to others' lives.

4. Don't jump to options.

Now that you have accepted that a career is a long game, and your identity is not defined by your career, the immediate next thought is: what are the next steps? What are my options?

We all have been taught to immediately get into a problem-solving action mode. The faster we solve a problem, the better incentives we receive.

Let's take the example of someone who wants to lose weight. When a friend recently found out that his cholesterol levels were a little high, the doctor recommended he lose some weight to bring it under control. So, he did what most of us would do—he joined a gym and went on a strict diet.

For a few weeks, he was very disciplined about what he ate and his exercise routine. From someone who ate late and loved his fried snacks, he went on to eating only salads and eating early.

Two weeks later, work pressure took over. He was eating late again, and usually unhealthy food. He would go to sleep late, which meant he ended up missing his morning gym sessions. He lost the motivation and zeal to manage his new diet and rigorous gym routine. He felt that he didn't have what it takes to become healthy. He resigned to the idea of popping pills to manage his BP and cholesterol.

We all have done this and know of people who do this. We immediately jump to action. We rely solely on motivation and will power to sustain a lifestyle change. When we are unable to keep it up, we label ourselves as 'indisciplined' or 'lazy'. Or, we say 'I hate diets' or 'I can never lose weight'.

Of course, this section is not about weight loss and healthy eating. This is a typical example of jumping into 'action mode' without allowing ourselves to get off the treadmill and pause!

In the context of your career, if we lose our job, we immediately search for a new one. We apply everywhere, frantically and crazily, without pausing. But Lochan tells her clients: 'Don't jump to options!'

When trying to reset your career, the first step is to understand our current reality. Before we start listing the different things we need to do, we need to identify, understand and accept where we currently are in terms of skills, mindset, life stage, financial comfort, abilities and priorities. This will help us make the transformation. We will explore this at length in Chapter 6.

Exercise 3: Value Wheel for Assessing Your Current Career Stage

Value wheel is an exercise we do to understand where the imbalance is coming from.

There are two versions shared here. One is to view the entire value wheel from a professional lens and understand where the imbalance is coming from. Another view is to look at it from a personal perspective and understand what the challenge is.

When an individual pauses to assess and evaluate the different dimensions of their life, they are able to understand what is causing their burnout. There are templates available online and you can choose to use those as well.

We have provided two templates for you to use.

THE WHEEL IS A SELF-COACHING ACTIVITY THAT WILL HELP YOU GET A 360-DEGREE VIEW OF YOUR CURRENT PROFESSIONAL SITUATION.

THE PURPOSE OF THIS ACTIVITY IS THREE-FOLD:

1. HELP YOU PAUSE AND REFLECT ON YOUR CURRENT WORK-LIFE
2. GUIDE YOU TO BUILD AN AGENDA/ FOCAL POINT FOR AREAS THAT NEED IMMEDIATE ATTENTION
3. ALLOW YOU TO REFLECT AND DEFINE YOUR GOALS BETTER

LET'S GET STARTED!

Template 1

Step 1: Fill out each slice of the wheel. You can also add/edit the headers.

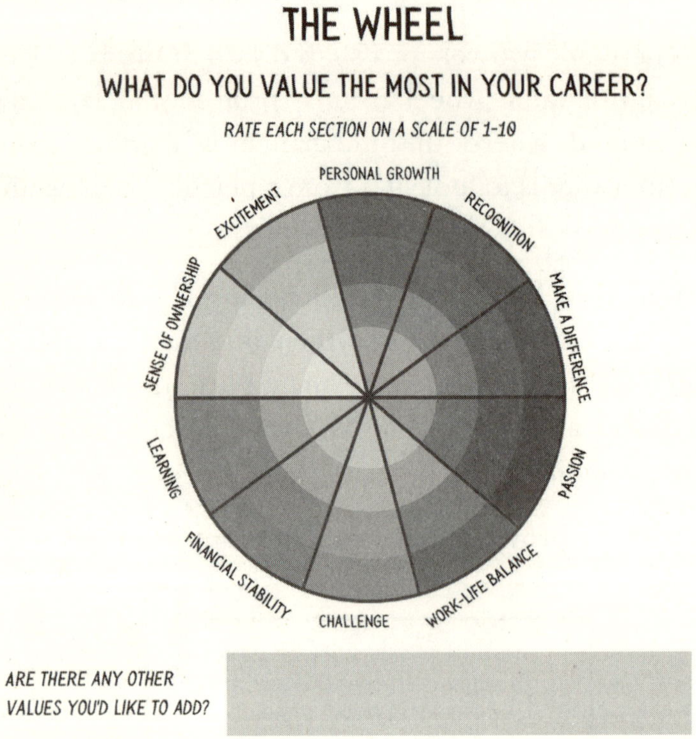

Step 2: Once you fill the details, think of the ideal work situation that you would like and map your current situation against it.

This immediately helps you identify areas that are important to you but not available in your current role. This may need some tweaks and changes in the current work that you are doing.

RATE THE VALUES IN AN IDEAL WORK SITUATION VS. YOUR CURRENT WORK SITUATION

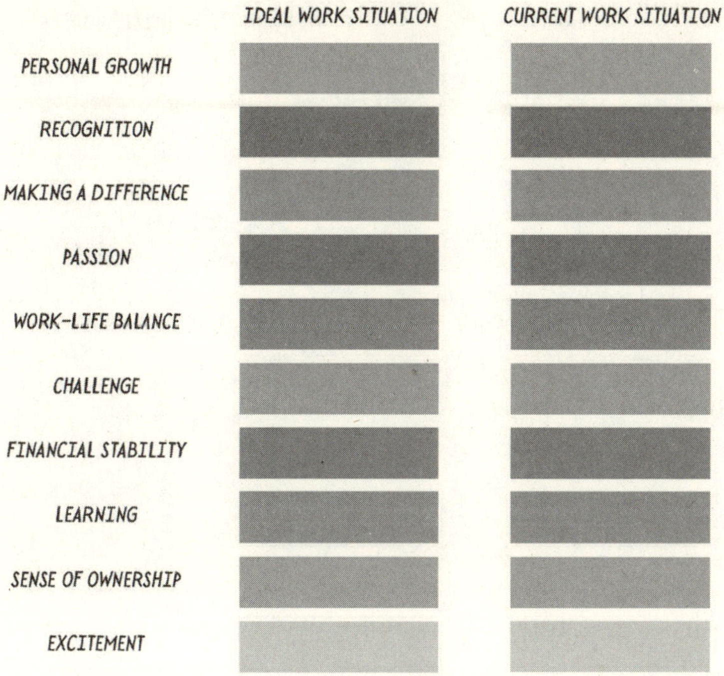

Step 3: Look at which of these factors are most present and least present in a particular aspect of your work.

This will help you narrow down on the area that is the cause of most concern to you, and how to handle the same better or identify which aspect needs to change.

Maybe you need to move to a new project with a different client, or work is great but the manager relationship is what is bothering you.

WHICH OF THESE VALUES ARE THE MOST AND LEAST REPRESENTED IN THE FOLLOWING AREAS:

WORK		PEER AND CLIENT RELATIONSHIPS	
MOST	LEAST	MOST	LEAST
E.G.: CHALLENGE	E.G.: PASSION		

MANAGER RELATIONSHIP		ORGANISATION CULTURE	
MOST	LEAST	MOST	LEAST

Step 4: Once you have identified where the challenge is more dominant, you can look at what could be the potential options to get out of this.

BASED ON YOUR VALUE RATINGS, ANSWER THE FOLLOWING QUESTIONS:

1. WHAT CAN YOU DO TO IMPROVE RATINGS IN YOUR CURRENT WORK?

2. WHAT DO YOU NEED TO CHANGE IN YOUR CAREER TO MAKE IT IDEAL?

3. WHAT EXTERNAL SUPPORT/ HELP DO YOU NEED?

Template 2

This is to gain an overall understanding of the gaps in any aspect of your life. This isn't restricted to only work but looks at life overall, including family, purpose, health, spirituality, etc.

Even as the template changes, the approach remains the same.

Step 1: Fill out each spoke of the wheel. You can also add/edit the headers.

THE WHEEL

WHAT DO I VALUE THE MOST?

RATE EACH SECTION ON A SCALE OF 1-10

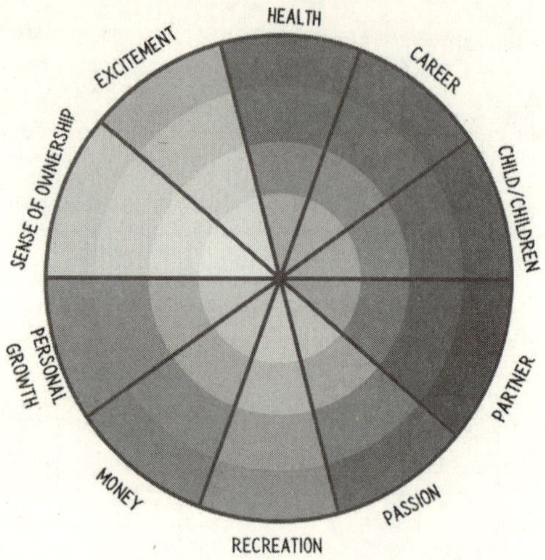

ARE THERE ANY OTHER VALUES YOU'D LIKE TO ADD?

Step 2: Once you fill out these details, think of the ideal situation that you would like and where are you against it today.

This immediately helps you identify areas that are important to you but not available in your current reality.

RATE THE AMOUNT OF ATTENTION YOU'D GIVE THESE DIMENSIONS IN AN IDEAL WORK SITUATION VS. HOW MUCH YOU GIVE YOUR CURRENT WORK SITUATION

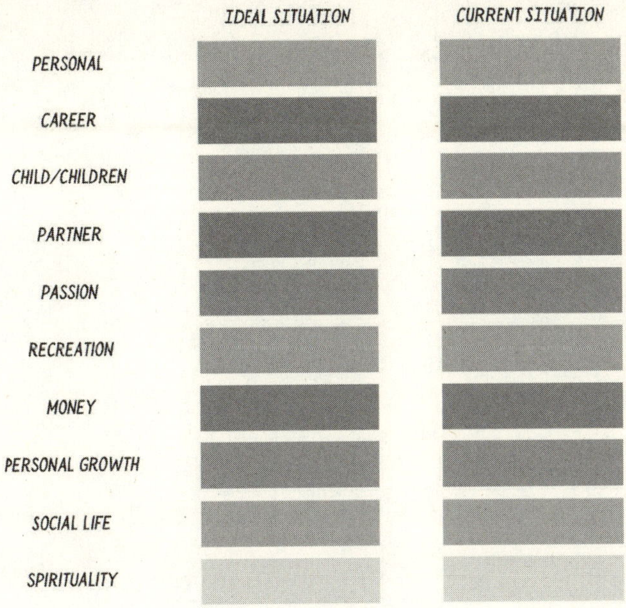

Step 3: Once you have identified what areas have the widest gaps, think of a few changes that you can make to improve them.

For example, if it is a relationship, then you make on a date with your partner once a month. If it is health, then you can add a daily walk of at least fifteen minutes to your routine.

BASED ON YOUR VALUE RATINGS, ANSWER THE FOLLOWING QUESTIONS:

1. WHAT DIMENSIONS ON MY WHEEL REQUIRE MORE ATTENTION?

2. WHAT DO I NEED TO CHANGE IN MY LIFE/CAREER TO MAKE IT IDEAL?

3. WHAT EXTERNAL SUPPORT/ HELP DO I NEED?

Key Takeaways

- Remember that your career is a long journey.
- Shifting perspectives in careers is important at all stages.
- Career goals, priorities and careers themselves can shift every decade. It's okay!
- Focus on building skills and look at your career shift from a skills perspective.
- If you don't take charge of your career, someone else will drive you to a destination that you don't want to go to!

chapter three

Will There Be Just One Perfect Role for You?

THE WORD 'CAREER' ORIGINATED IN THE SIXTEENTH century to denote a short gallop by a horse at a racecourse. The word originates in the Latin word 'carrus', which means wagon, and came into English from French. Before the twentieth century, the word 'career' referred to any continuous course of action or progress. However, as society evolved, the word's meaning changed. It now refers to one's professional life. What is interesting to note is that the initial meaning of the word aligns with the mindset of the young professional generation. This generation looks for action and progress. Often, they connect their career to constant change. New-age professionals have discovered the true meaning of the word 'career' at a philosophical level.

When Apoorv was working on his first venture, Startup Safari, in 2015, he saw how new-age professionals were evolving. Many founding team members were quitting, and he thought the reason could be poor work culture or stagnated growth. He was surprised when a team member told him the reason: 'I am at the hop on hop off stage of my career.' For those who have travelled across Europe and America, you would be very familiar with this bus ride. It's a sightseeing pass where you pay for the day, take any bus, get on and off wherever you like. Buying the ticket doesn't mean you have to stick to one bus; you can hop on another bus after exploring the place you got off at. Today, professionals are open to exploring; they can change the bus (company) or even the path (career path). They are not ready for a destination yet.

This has been a growing trend. It's one of the biggest evolutions in careers in the last five years. More and more of us look at our professional life as a hop-on hop-off bus. We do this until we figure out a worthwhile destination. We are ready to risk not having a job. Today, being settled is often equated with being stagnant in one's professional journey.

Nowadays, people are open to exploring different roles or handling multiple roles together. One such revelation was Neha, who would end up stepping in and taking charge each time something came up at work. Neha joined Apoorv's team as an intern with the intention of putting her passion for product development to practice. She carried with her a deep interest in learning and challenging her skill set at every step. Not only did she handle the entire programme management vertical, she also designed and created the product marketing strategy and led stakeholder management for the biggest clients. She was not an expert in all these aspects, but she enjoyed wearing different hats and had an insatiable desire to learn and grow. With her jack-of-many-trades quality, she became an asset to the team, where she could overlook product management, marketing and customer success.

Companies need multi-skilled employees who can boost cross-team collaboration. Most products aren't built in isolation, anyway. Multipotentialites often become key resources for companies.

What is Multipotentiality?

A psychological term, multipotentiality refers to a person's ability and preference to excel in two or more different fields. In simple terms, it's the antidote to being a specialist.

While in today's times, people often specialise in one field when it comes to their career, in the past, multipotentiality was common. We followed many interests and built a 'profession' around them. We were not defined or destined for a linear career path. During the Renaissance era, being a multipotentialite was the way to be. The leading thought leaders explored many skills and activities. The industrial age led to a shift in cultural norms, which now favour specialisation.

Let's explore this a bit more. Multipotentialites have no 'one true calling' the way specialists do. Being a multipotentialite becomes your destiny itself. You end up accessing many paths and pursuing them all, either one after another or at the same time—or both. These professionals thrive on learning, exploring and mastering new skills. Multipotentialites have multiple callings and tend to change professions over their lives. They choose a range of interests and paths over their lifetime. The list of famous multipotentialites might surprise you. We know them for one popular field of work. To name a few: Aristotle, Leonardo Da Vinci, Thomas Jefferson, Cleopatra, Eleanor Roosvelt and Gloria Steinem.

Multipotentiality: A Modern-day Career Story

Let's look at a real-life example of multipotentiality. Recently, we spent some time with a self-confessed multipotentialite and we were very intrigued by her journey. On the face of it, you might think of her as a job hopper or a freelancer. And those would be fair labels to judge her on but as we dug deep into her story, we started to see the curious world of multipotentiality and how it is becoming the reality for so many professionals post the COVID-19 pandemic.

Petra has an interesting career change story, that shows how an individual can go through life and overcome its challenges by making themselves flexible and open to using their skills and talents.

For Petra, an opportunity for changing her career path presented when she was made redundant from her job as accounting administrator. Though it was a forced change from a job she loved, Petra used it to explore multiple passions and skills. She experienced life as a chocolate taster (yes, that's correct!), French teacher, dog sitter and lately as a customer success associate for a health-tech company. And she is still dreaming of becoming a barista!

Let's explore Petra's journey through excerpts from a conversation Apoorv had with her about her career adventures.

Early Life: Interests and Education

What is your educational background?

I studied accountancy and foreign languages (English and French) in the Netherlands.

How many languages do you speak?

I speak Dutch, my native language, English, French and some German. I have always liked foreign languages. I would love to learn Russian and Japanese and would cherish the opportunity to travel and practise those languages.

What difference has the knowledge of these languages made in your life?

Learning English has helped me to find rewarding jobs and to settle down and integrate in the UK. It has broadened my mind and allowed me to be part of a multicultural community.

Which job did you want to do when you were a child?

I have always had lots of interests and can't remember exactly what I wanted to do. I went through a phase of wanting to become a mechanic and then a doctor.

Professional Life: Accounting Administrator and Redundancy

How did you become an accounting administrator?

I worked for a large financial company for over twelve years, initially in life insurance and then in administration. I started off working full time and then reduced my hours when I had my son in 2007. The company operated a flexi-working system and they were very supportive of working parents. Sadly, I was made redundant in 2012.

So, you were made redundant and lost a job you love. How did you feel at the time?

I felt disappointed and disheartened. The company gave us plenty of warning (they told us about the redundancies one year in advance), and they also paid for us to go on CV writing and job interview courses, which were extremely helpful. Consequently, the vast majority of my colleagues, including myself, managed to find jobs straightaway.

What did you do after your redundancy?

For the following four years, I worked for two companies, as a full-time administrator. The long hours, the unmanageable deadlines, the lack of training and support and the stressful environment took a toll on me, so much so that I decided to leave and never go back to accounting again, despite my extensive experience and good salary.

Overcoming Fear and Managing Different Jobs

Where did you go after leaving that job?

I was frightened and I had not realised my full potential and, initially, finding another job was extremely difficult. Surprisingly, my career path took lots of different directions as I started taking on different part-time jobs in disparate fields ranging from education to sensory evaluation and e-commerce, just to mention a few. After a few months of searching, I started a part-time job, working eight hours per week, as a sensory panellist, initially tasting gum and candy, then cocoa beverages and chocolate, for a large confectionery company. Yes, I know what you are thinking, getting paid to eat chocolate? That sounds like a dream job, and indeed it was.

At the same time, I advertised as a private French tutor and quickly found some students, so I was teaching both adults and teenagers and spreading my love for languages. Those two jobs were not enough for me, so, after a few months, I managed to find a part-time position as a customer service advisor in an e-commerce firm selling music merchandise.

Transferable Skills: The Secret Sauce of a Multipotentialite

What life and transferable skills have you learnt from these jobs?

I discovered that I could adapt quickly to new environments and could work with people from different backgrounds while communicating successfully with everyone. Being a multipotentialite allows me to perform a variety of roles throughout the day, and push my boundaries. I especially enjoyed the one-to-one relationship with my students. Also, the fact that they passed their French exams made me feel very proud. Building a portfolio of regular 'furry' clients in my dog-sitting job has also been enormously gratifying; I love dogs, and I understand how people find working with animals so rewarding.

Starting from Zero Again: New Beginnings

How and when did you start thinking about changing your career again?

I started considering a new career (another one?) a couple of years ago. The confectionery company I worked for decided to move to another town, and the news was heartbreaking for everyone! Initially,

I decided to stay on and give it a go. But the travel was too much and it helped me make a decision. I wrote down a list of pros and cons and finally decided it was time to move on.

What challenges did you have to overcome to start your new career?

I didn't want to go back to accounting; however, I thought my experience in financial services would help me open up a new path, and I applied for a full-time position as a client success associate for a health-tech company. Passing all the three interview stages was a challenge in itself; for the final interview, I was told I had to prepare a presentation. This took me by surprise as the job description did not mention it.

In the end, I decided to turn the presentation into a game. It's a method that motivates students to learn by using video game design and game elements in learning environments. I sometimes use it with my students to make learning more fun and interactive. Luckily my gamble paid off! I started a few weeks later, and I must admit the first few months were a real challenge. I worked very hard to learn how to use the software tools sold by the company so that I could fully support clients and colleagues alike. The role also involved delivering online webinars and training to clients and, despite my initial fears, I excelled in this field.

What Now: Exploring Multiple Interests as a Multipotentialite

Where do you see yourself in the future? What are you enjoying the most?

There is still some variety in my working life even though I only have one student now and have cut down on dog-sitting appointments. Ideally, I would prefer to work part-time again, perhaps in five or six years. Because I still have a keen interest in sensory evaluation, I would consider becoming a qualified barista. I have also recently signed up for an online course in social media marketing, which I am planning to complete by the end of the summer. I love online learning as it's very flexible and can be done from the comfort of your home.

On Evolving Careers When You Are a Multipotentialite

Why do you think changing a career is a good thing?

Unless you are a specialist in your field, you can change your career as many times as you like or need to. Or you could have various careers at the same time. A few years ago, I discovered a fantastic website for people with different careers and projects in their lives. It's called puttylike.com, a home for multipotentialites! You can take the test and find out which type of multipotentialite you are; I am a simultaneous multipotentialite. This means that I can run different jobs and projects at the same time. You could be a sequential multipotentialite, someone who is changing from one job to the next. The website provides help and support; you can find guides on topics like how to write your CV when you have a portfolio career, or how to manage different projects at the same time.

For a long time, being multi-passionate has been seen as a disadvantage. One came to believe that having one specialisation was the only way to give your 100 per cent to something. Moreover, the moonlighting controversy that was the topic of debate a couple of years ago also added to this line of thinking. However, all we need to ensure is that we maintain professional ethics and are transparent about holding various jobs or side hustles. Multipotentialites have several advantages:

- They learn fast and with joy; they are self-driven and disciplined (when it comes to things they are interested in).
- They are enthusiastic and adaptable.
- Thinking outside the box and identifying new angles of looking at a subject come easily to them.
- They are capable of seeing the big picture.
- They have connections in different fields and they often create bridges between those fields, bringing specialists from different areas together.

So what does it take to be a multipotentialite?

- It all comes down to learning how to put your strengths to a good use. We are so very different, and that variety can be useful if we know how to use it.
- You have to make peace with the fact that you won't become super-specialised in any of the fields you are interested in. You prefer to know a bit from many things than everything about just one.
- You might not be a genius but you will be an avid learner, problem solver and, occasionally, maybe one of those that will bring some genius innovation. Because that's one of the biggest advantages of having multiple interests: you can combine knowledge from different domains in unique ways.

Key Takeaways

- Moving forward, you don't have to always lock yourself in one role. You can explore diverse areas of passion.
- New-age companies are on the lookout for multipotentialites, especially early stage funded start-ups. They need support and domain expertise. Yet, the founders are usually cash strapped and don't have the necessary expertise or time. They are open to have people work on multiple roles together or even have part-time leaders.

chapter four

Finding What's Right for You

IN THE TIMES WE LIVE IN, ALL OF US FACE MULTIPLE challenges on the career front. The first challenge is to choose a career from among the various choices available to us. The rapid pace of technological changes globally has resulted in several new careers which didn't exist till a few decades ago. For example, the roles of social media manager and digital content creator, which are hugely popular today, have come up only in the last decade or so. The second challenge is our expectation from a career, which has undergone a drastic change. We now look for faster growth, greater flexibility and regular feedback in our careers. We may often take up a role but find a few years later that it doesn't fit our changed life circumstances.

The idea of a perfect job is often a myth we hold on to. We might think of ourselves on a tropical island, earning a good salary by caring for the island and snorkelling all day. But the truth is, there is no perfect job. Some jobs may be a better fit for our skills and interests, but there will always be days when we lack motivation. Ultimately, our job satisfaction depends on how much effort we put in and our willingness to get better. So instead of searching for the perfect job, we should focus on making the most of the job we have.

Not all dream jobs involve travelling to amazing places, playing music or giving speeches. When you think about your ideal role, consider these five important elements.

Five Key Ingredients of Your Ideal Role

1. Work that's engaging

What matters is not your salary, status, type of company, and so on, but rather, what you do day-by-day, hour-by-hour. Researchers have identified four factors, the most empirically verified predictors of work satisfaction:

1. The freedom to decide how to perform your work
2. Clear tasks, with a defined start and end
3. Variety in the types of tasks
4. Feedback, so you know how well you're doing.

2. Work you enjoy

It's not the sparkles or glitters of perks/benefits that will hold you to a role for a long time. Are you enjoying the real grunt work in day-to-day tasks? If your answer to this is yes, then it's the right role for you.

3. Work you're good at

Being good at your work makes you feel great. It boosts your confidence and helps you negotiate for other good things in your role, like working on exciting projects, doing interesting tasks and getting paid fairly. If your work is valued, you can ask for these things in your employment agreement.

4. Work that fits with the rest of your life

It's not necessary to rely solely on your work to achieve a fulfilling life. You can find ways to make ends meet with a role while also excelling at a side project, finding purpose through philanthropy and volunteering, or cultivating meaningful relationships outside of work.

5. Lack of major negatives

To achieve work satisfaction, it's not only necessary to have the positive aspects mentioned earlier, but also the absence of factors that make work unpleasant. The following are typically associated with work dissatisfaction:

- A lengthy commute, particularly if it takes over an hour
- Excessively long working hours
- A feeling of being underpaid
- Job insecurity

This is an ingredient people underestimate. In the search of optimising the positives, we may also expand the negatives.

We can learn from Sarika's journey. She started out her career at a top IT services company and quickly realised that coding was not for her. While coding was not her forte, she was excellent at customer management. After taking up project management roles, she eventually decided to move to a pre-sales role. Soon she realised that while pre-sales was considered a prestigious role, it required long working hours, deep technical expertise and frequent deadlines. With a small child who kept getting sick, the job became too difficult for her to handle. It just didn't fit in with the rest of her life and resulted in work dissatisfaction. She was soon looking for another role.

Determine which ingredients are currently in your career path and which are missing. If an ingredient is important to you, then it's time to find ways to incorporate it into your life. Once you have identified which ingredients are important for you and what kind of roles meet those ingredients, it is time to find that role.

Finding Your Ideal Role

Discovering one's ideal job is not easy. A good way to do it is to try different things to figure out what fits in your life scheme. There are many tools available that can help you in your journey of career pivoting. You may use tools to find out more about your values.

You can take advantage of:

- *VIA tool*: The VIA tool is a free self-assessment that takes ten minutes. It provides you a wealth of information that helps you identify your character strengths.
- *360-degree feedback mechanisms*: The 360-degree feedback, which was discussed in detail in Chapter 1, helps identify your strengths and blind spots.
- *Journaling*: Journaling allows introspection. It helps answer questions like how you are feeling right now. It also helps identify areas where you may need to make changes. Journaling prompts self-reflection. It can also help you weigh the advantages and disadvantages of making a pivot.
- *Mentorship sessions*: Talk to your mentors about your career to get their perspective. Specifically, seek out individuals who have known you professionally for a long time. (This has been discussed in Chapter 1.)

Alternatively, we have developed a framework to shortlist career options. BRUSH is a framework that we have created to work with our coachees/mentees. This is specifically relevant for younger professionals at the early juncture of their career. It can also be useful to professionals who have never made a career/job shift.

Use the BRUSH Framework to Get More Career Clarity

Step 1: **B** – Build a list of options.

Step 2: **R** – Rank the options.

Step 3: **U** – Uncertainties preparedness.

Step 4: **S** – Start research.

Step 5: **H** – Have an action plan.

Step 1: Make a list of options

Write down your initial list. Include the problem you want to focus on and the role you want.

Here are some questions to help you think of more:

- If you could take any of the options on your initial list, what would you do?
- If money were no object, what would you do?
- What do your friends advise?
- If experienced, how could you use your most valuable skills?
- Can you combine your options to make the best of both worlds?
- Can you find any more opportunities through your connections?
- What did you enjoy doing most?

You may enjoy sleeping and watching movies, but it's unlikely you can make money from them. Answer these questions from a skills perspective.

Step 2: Rank your options

1. Start by making an initial guess.
2. If you have more time, then score your options from one to five, based on the following parameters:
   - impact
   - personal fit
   - other elements of job satisfaction
   - any other factors that are important to you.
3. Then try to cut down to a shortlist. Eliminate the options that are worse on all factors than another, and those that are very poor on one factor. You can add up all your scores to get a very rough ranking of options. If one of your results seems odd, try to understand why. For each option, ask yourself: 'Why might I be wrong?' Adjust your ranking. This is a very useful way to reduce bias.

Step 3: Pre-empt uncertainties

What information could most easily change your ranking? If you could get the answer to one question, which question would be most useful? Write these out. For example, 'Can I get a place on Teach for India?',

'Would I enjoy programming?', 'How pressing is climate change compared to open science?'. If you're unsure, picture having to choose your career in only one weekend. What actions would you take during that time to ensure you made the correct decision?

Step 4: Start research

This is a critical step and comes before you take action. Generic research doesn't help make a clear decision. Instead make your research specific. This ensures you have all the necessary information to make an informed decision. Ensure you talk to two or three people in the same field but in a different industry or type of organisation. This will give you a realistic estimate of what to expect.

For example, if you're unsure whether you'll enjoy being a data scientist, find someone you could talk to about what it's like. Don't just ask them: 'Is data science a good career option?' Instead ask them questions about what their day-to-day work looks like, what kind of projects they are working on, how much autonomy they get in their role, what career progression looks like in their field, what kind of responsibilities someone starting their career in the field will have, and so on.

Step 5: Have an action plan

Once you have ranked your options, managed the uncertainties and done your research, it is time to take action. The action plan involves you taking the step towards that particular role or career path.

The action plan could involve an additional course, a side project or an internship. In an organisation, you could also check for stretch assignments, short-term assignments or cross-functional opportunities to explore the field better.

Individual development plan (IDP), personal development plan, career goal setting, etc. are some formats that different organisations use to gain a better understand of the interests of their employees. In addition, you could also express your interest in other areas during your performance review discussions or look at opportunities within the company through internal job postings.

Exercise 4: BRUSH Framework to Choose Your Career Options

Step 1: Make a list of options

List down all the different roles you may like to explore or roles you can be good at. It can be as varied as being a data scientist and a wildlife photographer.

Tip: At this point, don't qualify and just write your wish list of careers. Aim to fill out at least twenty.

S. No.		S. No		S. No	
1		11		21	
2		12		22	
3		13		23	
4		14		24	
5		15		25	
6		16		26	
7		17		27	
8		18		28	
9		19		29	
10		20		30	

Step 2: Rank your options

2.a Rank them based on a hunch/intuition.

Give them a score between 1 and 5, with 5 being the highest and 1 being the lowest.

S. No.		Rank (1–5)	S. No		Rank (1–5)
1			16		
2			17		
3			18		
4			19		
5			20		
6			21		
7			22		
8			23		
9			24		
10			25		
11			26		
12			27		
13			28		
14			29		
15			30		

2.b Rank them based on the following parameters.

Look at the ones with a score of more than 3.

Give them a score between 1 and 5, with 5 being the highest and 1 being the lowest on each parameter. For the parameter 'Any other', please mention one other parameter critical for you (for instance, city-specific, global mobility, work-life balance, hustle, etc.)

Provide a total score at the end.

Remove the ones with a score less than 12.

S. No.		Monetary benefit	Personal fitment	Suitable environment	Sense of purpose	Any other	Total score
1							
2							
3							
4							
5							
6							
7							
8							
9							
10							
11							
12							
13							
14							

S. No.		Monetary benefit	Personal fitment	Suitable environment	Sense of purpose	Any other	Total score
15							
16							
17							
18							
19							
20							

Step 3: Uncertainty preparedness

Once you have made a shortlist of roles, evaluate them from the different uncertainties that can stop you from doing the role. We have given some questions for you to consider. You may like to add to this list.

S. No.	Questions	Your answers
1	What information will change my ranking?	
2	Which from the above is the most important factor for me?	

S. No.	Questions	Your answers
3	Will I enjoy ____ ______________ ______________? (fill in with all the roles one by one and answer)	
4	Which of the factors am I willing to compromise on?	
5	Will I be influenced by what my friend(s) will opt for?	
6	What would I not like in a role or work environment?	
7	What kind of career prospects does ________ role have?	
8	How different is ______ role from my current role?	

S. No.	Questions	Your answers
9	How comfortable am I to learn something completely new or from scratch?	
10	How much time can I spend to learn something new or refresh my learning at this stage of my life?	

Step 4: Start research

Once you have your shortlist, start the research to know more about it. We have shared a list of questions that you can ask. You can add you own questions as well.

S. No.	Questions	Your answers
1	What information do I need to make a decision?	

S. No.	Questions	Your answers
2	Who can help me make a decision?	
3	Do I know someone in that industry who can provide more information—a senior, a mentor, etc.?	
4	What are some of the questions that I would like to ask this person?	
5	What information will help me make a decision?	
6	Can I watch videos and get more information?	

S. No.	Questions	Your answers
7	Can I attend some free courses and understand it for myself?	
8	Can I speak to a career counsellor and get this information?	

Step 5: Have an action plan

Once you have shortlisted three or four roles that you will find interesting, you can use some of the below questions as guiding questions to understand more. You can add more questions to this list.

S. No.	Questions	Your answers
1	Can I do a project in this field?	
2	Can I take up a part-time internship?	

S. No.	Questions	Your answers
3	Can I explore some pro bono assignments along with my current role?	
4	Which forums or groups will help me learn more about this field? Can I join them?	
5	Can I look for internal job postings for this kind of role?	
6	Can I speak to my managers/ mentors to understand how to make this switch internally?	

S. No.	Questions	Your answers
7	Can I apply for short-term assignments or projects to explore this field better?	
8	Are there cross-functional projects that can help me get a better idea of the work in this field?	

Should You Be Following Your Passion?

'Find a job you love, and you will never have to work a day in your life ...'

All of us have heard this phrase and set out to find the job we love. Here comes the concept of passion or IKIGAI.

It is often said that following your passion or IKIGAI is good advice for choosing a career. A lot of professionals are struggling to either convert their passion into their career or find passion in their career. The result is a lot of frustration, dissatisfaction and disengagement.

Recent studies[1] show that prioritising happiness as the main goal in life can actually make us less happy and have negative effects. Instead of just seeking happiness, it is more beneficial to pursue a sense of purpose, also known as the 'purpose path'.

In their article titled 'Your Job Doesn't Have to Be Your Passion', Lauren C. Howe, Jon M. Jachimowicz and Jochen I. Menges throw light on this important job vs passion debate.

> The pandemic has been a wake-up call for a lot of people, causing us to reevaluate our lives and our careers. It's natural to think: 'If I'm going to spend so much time at work, I might as well do something I'm passionate about.' But there are also benefits to thinking about it differently. Instead of pursuing a

career based on your passion, how can your career help you pursue your passion?

Having a passion outside of work is less risky. Some research suggests that turning hobbies into work can make you enjoy them less.

Instead, look for a job that will give you the resources—time, money, and energy—to pursue your passion.

If time is your scarcest resource, look for a job that offers schedule flexibility so that you can structure your work around your passions.

If money is the issue, look for a job that allows you to pay for the life you want to lead.

When it comes to energy, don't think of your passion as something that provides fuel to energise you for work. Instead, look at your job as giving you the security and income to pursue your passion.[2]

When you pursue a career you love, it can bring you benefits like better job performance, job satisfaction and higher earnings. However, there are also trade-offs. It is important to weigh the pros and cons of pursuing your passion through work. Instead of asking 'How can I find a job that I'm passionate about?', try asking 'How can my career be a conduit to passion?'

You can pursue your passion outside of work. This is less risky and helps you set boundaries between your work and personal lives. It also lets you meet like-minded people who can give you insight into what your day-to-day would be like if you turned your passion into your job. If you choose not to pursue your passion at work, find a job that gives you the time, money and energy to pursue your passions.

'By trying to monetise my passion, I found a waning interest in my passion.' This is what Dipti, a young professional in a start-up, had to say. Post her graduation, she was figuring out what to do. Since she was a fantastic artist, friends and family suggested that she take up art full time. She started to put up her work at shows and getting commissioned work but soon found herself tired and overwhelmed with her work. Art had always brought her joy. It had been her stress buster and she kept experimenting with different styles only to suit her interest. Once she started to monetise it and make a profession out of it, the joy she felt began to wane. She had to work on what others wanted, leaving her with little or no time to do her own art. What had once been a stress buster quickly became a cause of stress for her. She eventually joined a young start-up. She took charge of their marketing and social media. She was able to use her passion for research and art effectively. She still pursues her art on the side and takes occasional commissioned work. However, she has chosen to not make her career in art. Instead, she has chosen a career that can feed and support her passion for art.

As you are navigating your career, turning your passion into a profession may not always provide you with the desired success. In turn, keeping the two separate may actually create a more fulfilling and purposeful life.

Some questions for you to reflect on:

- How can my career be a *conduit* to passion?
- Which industries will allow me to pursue my passion?
- Do the constraints of these industries align or conflict with my other goals? These goals include having a family, spending time on my hobbies, building wealth and choosing where I want to live.
- Do I *need* to pursue my passion through my work?
- What would it look like to pursue this passion outside work? Would it be equally fulfilling?
- Should you make your career your passion, or find a job that allows you to spend time on it outside work?
- Will this job give me the resources—meaning time, money and energy—to pursue my passions?

If you prioritise time as your most precious resource, you may enjoy seeking a job that offers a flexible and predictable schedule.

But, if money is your main concern, it's essential to find a job that provides the financial means to support the lifestyle you desire. If you have expensive hobbies or interests, your job can help you afford them. It is especially important to consider the specific circumstances, especially in countries like India where there is no social security and only your family and friends can provide support in times of need.

Key Takeaways

1. Five key ingredients of your ideal role are:
    - Work that's engaging
    - Work you enjoy
    - Work you're good at
    - Work that fits with the rest of your life
    - Lack of major negatives
2. Use the BRUSH framework to get more career clarity
    - Step 1: B – Build a list of options
    - Step 2: R – Rank the options
    - Step 3: U – Uncertainty preparedness
    - Step 4: S – Start research
    - Step 5: H – Have an action plan
3. Following your passion is not going to work for everybody, especially in countries like India, where there is no social security and only your family and friends can provide support in times of need. You can also pursue your passion outside work. This is less risky and helps you set boundaries between your work and personal life.

chapter five

How to Land Your Dream Job Without Quitting?

LINKEDIN CEO RYAN ROSLANSKY SAYS, 'I TRULY BELIEVE that your next top employee is most likely your current employee. And if you focus on skills and understand the skills of your existing workforce, and where you need to go as a company, there's a huge opportunity to help your top talent find different roles inside of your company instead of learning and leaving. Our data shows that at the two-year mark, an employee who has made an internal move has a 75% likelihood of staying as opposed to the mere 56% likelihood for an employee who hasn't made an internal move.'[1]

If you dislike your job because it doesn't align with your skills, you could miss out on opportunities by quitting without exploring other positions within the company. For instance, Paridhi completed her chemical engineering degree in 2008 from Pune. Since the jobs in the core sector were few, she took up a campus placement for a role in a leading IT services company. She quickly realised she enjoyed not the technical side but the business side of things. She moved to a business analyst role internally, eventually becoming a partner programme manager. She has been with the same organisation for over fourteen years, in a job she truly enjoys. It would have been a loss if she had quit without even exploring an internal change.

A lot of organisations provide their employees the option of taking a sabbatical, or to go for integrated learning; some even sponsor higher education of their employees. Before you decide to leave, explore these options in your organisation. Looking at your company's website, especially the employee benefits section, or talking to your HR business partner can be a good starting point.

You may wonder how to determine if your organisation will allow an internal job change and support you in a new role. You can consider a couple of pointers to check this objectively:

- Look for existing examples where employees in your organisation have made such moves. If there is precedence then it makes your case stronger.
- Contact your HR business partner to learn about the company's policies for supporting employees in transitioning between roles. Most forward-thinking companies have internal job posting systems that make such a move possible.
- Your organisation can help you bridge the gap between your current role and your desired role.

They can do this by providing in-house training, sponsoring training or education programmes, or offering a sabbatical.

- Look for people within your organisation who can be your mentor/coach/sponsor for this cause

Five Ways to Make an Internal Move

Navigating the maze of a large organisation is often challenging. Despite working in an organisation for many years, most individuals don't get to know about other teams, departments or even people. Thus, sometimes, being able to make an internal move feels more challenging than moving out of the organisation. Here are some ways that can help you make an internal move.

1. Take up side projects

A big advantage of working in a large progressive company is your ability to switch streams in your career. It may take time but it's worth the wait. Gaurav spent ten years working in an IT role starting as a developer and eventually moving up to become a project manager. But this role was not bringing him joy. He wanted to switch to an HR role but he did not have a formal HR degree. So he started to gain experience by volunteering as a technical panellist in the company's campus recruitment drive. He enjoyed interacting with engineering students who were eager but didn't know much about getting a job in the IT industry. By volunteering, he learnt the basics of the role and gained some valid experience to apply for an internal move in the HR function.

2. Check sponsored courses

Companies also offer paid courses, certifications, and sometimes work integrated degrees based on their benefit policy. You can check the company portal to see the options for seeking learning opportunities in your drcam rolc. Ramesh wanted to pursue a career in data science. He was chosen for a master's programme in data science by his company. His organisation sponsored a WILP (work integrated learning programme) that allowed him to study for a master's degree at a prestigious academic institute on weekends while still earning his salary.

3. Discuss your aspirations with HR and the leadership team

You can directly discuss your aspirations with HR and the leadership team. You'll be surprised to find out that such discussions are slowly becoming common where employees no longer want to stick to the roles that their degree destined them for. One such example is that of Girish, an operations head for a large e-commerce company. He had spent almost a decade and a half across operations, analytics and pricing roles. During one of his annual appraisal discussions, he brought up the desire to try a completely different vertical such as Finance or HR to get a holistic understanding of the business to his manager. Six months later, his manager shared an opening in HR with him; the Compensation & Benefits team rolled up the role to him. If he was interested in the role, his manager was willing to put in a word to the hiring manager. He applied and interviewed for the role and eventually moved as a HR leader. This role opened his perspective to the business at large and helped him hone his business acumen.

4. Network with different teams to explore opportunities

Many off-the-record opportunities are discussed internally (like how it happened in Girish's case), and your colleagues may put in a word for you. Gaurav helped his colleague Chaitanya get one such opportunity. Chaitanya told Gaurav that he wanted to switch from being an IT programmer in an internal organisation project to working as a business analyst. Gaurav immediately recalled a recent conversation with his previous project lead. She had a similar opening and was desperately looking for a suitable person. He connected with the project manager and referred Chaitanya for the role.

Chaitanya was selected for the role of a business analyst for a prestigious client project. A year later, this led him to visit North America for an assignment at the customer location. It also paved the path for his learning and future career growth. This role was not advertised internally. If he had not used a wider network, it would have been difficult and taken longer for him to make this career transition.

Chaitanya is a classic example of 'building luck into your career'. He met Gaurav by chance, but he took the opportunity to talk about his interests.

You don't have to limit yourself to your immediate colleagues. With social media, networking has blurred the borders of office premises.

5. Explore the option of a sabbatical to get a degree

With so many options available to make an internal move, we have kept taking a sabbatical as last. This is the right option when you have fewer financial responsibilities, or you are financially stable enough to afford a break. Also, you get admission to an institution that would be worth a break. In such cases, many companies provide two-year sabbaticals for you to pursue a degree and join back on completion.

Sumit joined a large IT services organisation as an entry-level software engineer. He worked for two and a half years. He realised that he enjoyed interacting with people more than sitting at his computer and would like to work as an HR rather than optimising code. He researched his options and discovered he could have the best of both worlds by taking a sabbatical. He ensured job security by taking unpaid leave to study for a two-year MBA programme in HR. He came back and joined the organisation in an HR role. His role was to lead campus hiring. He also got a higher salary when he changed his career path.

Minal's story is also inspiring. While working in a central government department, she got a chance to study a fully funded master's programme in Nuclear Safety at a leading university in South Korea. It would accelerate her career growth. But the dilemma was that she had a five-year-old child to take care of. But with the support of her family, she took this call, which eventually paid off in her long-term career. After her master's, she got exciting assignments, and currently, she works with the United Nations in a strategic global role.

Gaurav has also changed careers multiple times in the past eighteen years. He went from being a software developer to a business analyst and switched from IT to HR to Research and Innovation. All while staying in the same company.

He has learnt that making a big change requires taking a risk. You can easily use your transferable skills and leverage your network to easily change roles within the same organisation. People truly underestimate this aspect.

In the Indian context, attrition in the Indian IT industry touched 25 per cent in FY22.[2] Big IT organisations can have between three lakh and five lakh employees. This means that in one year, more than one lakh employees could leave a big IT organisation. Many of them could be moved internally and companies are open to discussion.

When you change companies, you have to learn to take on new responsibilities and adapt to a new work environment. If you stay in the same company, you already know how things work and are familiar with the company culture. You can always rejoin the company, but in such cases, the company treats you like an external hire. You still have to go through an interview and selection process, which might not result in a job offer. Staying in one organisation is also helpful in the long run.

N. Chandrasekaran is a great example of this. He joined TCS as an intern in 1987 and worked his way up to become the company's CEO in 2009. Eventually, in 2017, he became the chairman of Tata Sons. By staying in the same organisation and building his skills over time, he was able to achieve great success.

How to Get Internal Referrals Using LinkedIn

Apoorv was amused at the idea that you may need to use platforms like LinkedIn to connect with other employees in your company. This can be especially true for large organisations with over five thousand employees.

LinkedIn is a powerful tool for making internal transitions within your company. By connecting with colleagues and employees from different departments and locations, you can uncover new opportunities that align with your career aspirations. Take the example of

Raj, who worked in the HR department of a multinational corporation managing university partnerships. Raj wanted to transition to a research and innovation role but wasn't sure where to start. He revised his LinkedIn profile to highlight his university partnership management and stakeholder management skills. He then reached out to an innovation manager within his company through LinkedIn, asking for an informational interview. During their conversation, Raj learnt about an upcoming opening in the innovation team that would deal with university research. He received valuable advice on how to position himself for the role. This connection not only provided him with insights but also led to an internal referral, eventually helping him secure the position. The following steps can help you leverage LinkedIn to facilitate your internal career transition.

1. Revise your LinkedIn profile. Focus on your most notable achievements and provide specific examples. People who are interested in meeting you will review your profile.
2. If you know someone in your organisation who can hire you, then ask them for a meeting to discuss job openings in their department. This approach is like skipping the screening process and going straight to an interview. Remember, you don't have to wait for an open position because companies often create positions for capable people.
3. If you don't know the person well, you can ask for an informational interview to learn about job

opportunities in the industry. If the meeting goes well, you can ask them to introduce you to people who could hire you. This is called a referral. But if you agree to an informational interview, don't ask them for a job on their team.

4. When you want more introductions, be ready with a short, clear description of the specific opportunities you want to find. A good example is something like: 'a mid-level innovation position at a business unit in the finance sector'.

5. If the previous options are not available, try using the connections of the people you know. For example, if you have a close friend who knows an individual capable of hiring, you could ask your friend to refer you. The best option is to seek a referral from someone you have worked with in the past and had a positive performance evaluation.

6. If you have tried everything else and still can't make connections, it might help to build your network in the industry. You can start by contacting people with whom you have something in common, like alumni from your university or friends of friends. Your university may have a list of alumni who are willing to assist in different industries. You can also consider joining relevant groups and attending conferences to expand your network. If all else fails, you can resort to sending unsolicited emails to make cold connections.

Key Takeaways

- Consider making an internal move before quitting.
- Five ways to make an internal move are:
    - Take up side projects.
    - Check sponsored courses.
    - Discuss your aspirations with HR and the leadership team.
    - Network with different teams to explore opportunities.
    - Explore the sabbatical option to get the degree.

chapter six

How to Make Your Next Move?

WE WOULD LIKE TO BELIEVE THAT BY THE TIME YOU have reached here, you are thinking of making your next move. You have mentally aligned with the idea of exploring more avenues external to your organisation to make you feel unstuck. It is obviously not easy, and it requires a lot of effort on one's part to make this shift.

The Seven-Step Framework

To enable your move, you can follow the seven-step framework:

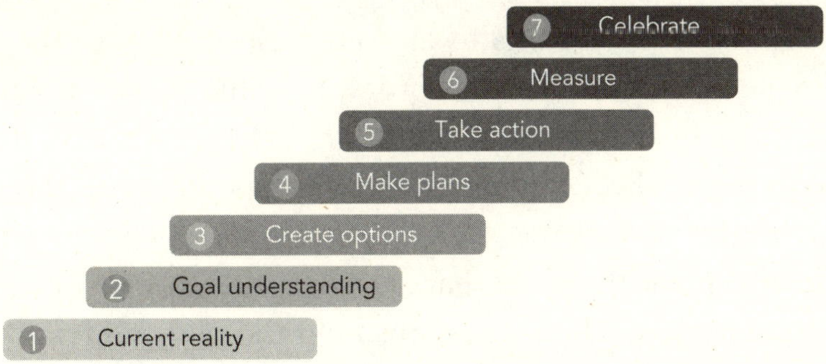

Let us try and understand this framework with the help of Ramya's story.

Ramya is a sales professional with eight years of experience. She is interested in exploring a marketing role but did not get an option to make an internal move. She decided to seek an opportunity externally.

Lochan did this exercise with Ramya and this is how these steps helped Ramya think through of her next move.

Step 1: What is my current reality today?

This question encompasses multiple facets. You can answer some of the following questions to get clarity on where you are in terms of your current reality:

- Do I know what my career drivers are—which type of work or environment do I prefer?
- Do I know what my greatest successes were and how I achieved them?
- What are my key skills?

When a person starts to answer these questions, they explore more about themselves. This helps them understand everything about their current state or current reality. A person needs to spend some time correctly identifying their current reality. They need to do this without the baggage of a title, a role or an organisation. These questions help the person identify what areas they want to keep and which they're okay to let go.

When Lochan did this exercise with Ramya, she started by helping Ramya understand her current reality.

- She enjoyed influencing people, negotiating with them and closing deals.
- She was not necessarily excited about the industry she was in but instead was more excited about the role and work she was doing.
- She did not enjoy building new teams and this part of her role was also really stressing her out.
- She was absolutely fine with relocating to a different city for the right job.
- She also created a list of skills she currently holds.

Ramya's circle of skills looked like this:

Step 2: Goal understanding

The second step is to understand, 'Where do you want to go?'

While the question 'Where do you see yourself five years from now' sounds passe, in this context, it is helpful. While trying to answer this question, adopt a holistic perspective. Some of the questions that you should ask yourself once you are in this step are as follows:

- In the next decade, what would you like to see yourself do more of?
- In the next decade, what do you see yourself doing less of?
- What kind of environment would you like to work in?
- What would you do if you had unlimited resources?
- How can you continue to use your best talent?
- Which roles are you targeting?

Such questions help you look at the future from the lens of your current reality. This enables you to create a goal or outlook for yourself. The reason this step comes after a check on the current reality is because it also provides clarity on what you want to do and what you don't want to do. In addition, it also immediately opens up your mind to look at areas that are not relevant anymore as well as new skills that you need to pick up.

Once Ramya had understood her current reality and understood what she wanted to continue doing, what her priorities were and the skills she had, it was time for her to look at the next step.

As Ramya answered some of these questions, she understood that:

- She is persuasive and wants to do more roles that involve communicating with customers.
- She is a team player and wants to work in a collaborative environment.
- She sees herself doing more of building a market or demand for something new.

Based on these revelations, she listed the roles she found interesting:

- Digital marketing manager
- Content strategist
- Paid campaigns specialist
- SEO specialist

She found the role of a digital marketing manager most interesting because of the wide variety of things she could do, all of which fall under the scope of digital marketing.

Step 3: Explore options

The next step is to create options—basically, how to get those roles. Let's explain this with Ramya's example.

After Ramya shortlisted the role she was targeting, she started the further discovery phase on how to get those roles. Was there any particular industry or domain she was interested in? In the past, she had worked mostly in the edtech industry. She was interested in continuing in the same industry. She further realised she could target entry-level roles, even do a two-month internship if needed, and then apply for a role.

In this step, she also explored how to become eligible for those roles. These questions helped her.

- What can you do to bridge this gap?
- What skills do you need to fill this gap?
- Who can help you?
- What information do you need to achieve your goal?
- Where can you get this information?

She mapped her current skillset and her required skillset and identified the overlap. The activity looked like this image:

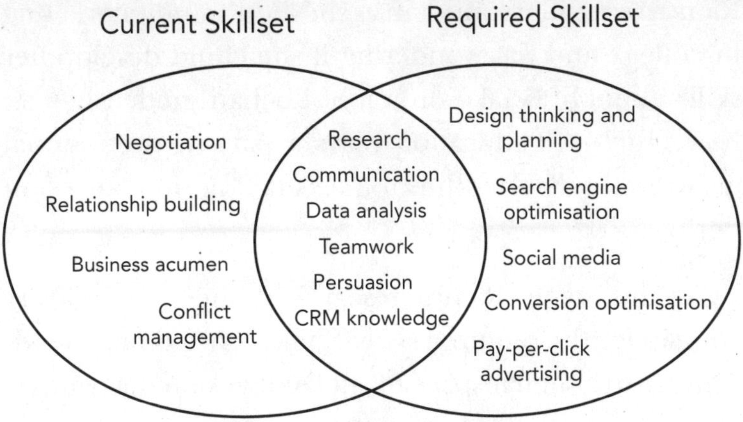

After Ramya finished this step, she had a clear idea of:

- The role she was targeting
- The domain or industries she is interested in
- A list of skills that she needed to develop.

She already possessed some of the required skills and she could look at some courses for the other skills. She also felt more confident as she was not starting from scratch.

Step 4: Prepare your action plan

After having clarity of the goal, it's time to create the action plan. The main things to cover in the action plan are:

- How to develop the required skills for the role
- How to apply for those roles.

Ramya was underconfident as she didn't study marketing in college and was wondering if she could develop her skills enough to take on a job. Lochan guided her on how much self-education plays a part in professional growth and directed her towards taking up courses on her own.

At this stage, Ramya researched the best industry courses for the required skills. She contacted her friends who are in a similar space to get feedback on the courses.

She also discussed with Lochan how to land these roles. While the usual job portals are an option, Lochan suggested using social media and networking to land the role.

Step 5: Take action

In the absence of action based on a well-laid-out plan, the first four steps will fall flat. Once the plan is in place, we need to act on it and be consistent with our efforts. Then we can start measuring the effectiveness of our actions and identifying the changes needed.

With a lot of difficulty, Ramya held back her need to 'jump to action'. She created an action plan and thought through all the potential roadblocks. She identified ways to deal with both intrinsic and extrinsic challenges. Once she got into the action phase, she spent six months completing the required courses. She also connected with people on social media. Ramya would do the following with the new connections she made:

- She would ask them more about their industry. She would explain her experience and skills in line with their industry. She would try to understand if their industry or organisations were the right place for her.
- She was able to narrow down companies that she could apply to.
- She started to find people in these companies and started building her network.
- Some of these people provided her information and even helped her to apply for suitable jobs. Some connections even guided her through the interview process.

By doing all this, Ramya gained confidence and clarity on what she had to offer and who valued it. The best part of Ramya's journey was when she found an accountability partner in Lochan who helped her stay motivated and stay on top of things.

Step 6: Measure yourself

'What doesn't get measured, doesn't improve'.

This old saying is also applicable in this case. In this step, we measure our effort and success. It answers this question: how will I know I am making progress?

In Ramya's case, she put both tangible and intangible measures. Her success metrics were:

- Number of courses completed
- Number of new relevant connections made
- Number of conversations or interviews landed.

Her first measure was how confident she felt in each interview. With each conversation and interview, she gained confidence about what she could bring to the role and the organisation. This helped her approach different individuals across organisations. Her initial conversations with prospective hiring managers started to get fruitful.

After a few months of efforts, Ramya landed a new role as a digital marketing executive for an edtech company in a new city.

Step 7: Celebrate

This is a last but crucial step. Every small milestone and achievement must be celebrated. That is what makes the journey worthwhile.

Any mountain climber will tell you that as much as they look ahead and walk, they occasionally look back to see how far they've come. This 'looking back' helps them see how much they have climbed and where they have reached.

Find your own ways of celebration:

- A pat on the back
- Public announcement of the achievement
- A small treat to yourself
- A celebration with your family and friends
- A simple 'I did it' poster on your wall!

This step is important and needs to be looked at purely from a lens of what you wanted to achieve and what you did manage to achieve. It doesn't have to be too big of an effort. For instance, in the case of Ramya, she decided to eat her favourite ice cream every time she completed a course or landed a new interview. Celebrating these small wins kept her motivated. Find that one thing you treat yourself with on hitting your mini goals.

You may face hurdles while following this seven-step framework. A perfect plan is bound to fail if it doesn't avoid the pitfalls. The typical pitfalls are:

- *Inertia*: Making a plan sounds great and helps one feel in control. But getting up and doing that activity consistently can feel cumbersome. There is inertia in challenging the status quo. We may not find support in our family. We have certain habits that are not supportive of this change. We have to get into a new habit that supports the action and any new habit requires some change. This change can be challenging.

- *Fear of the unknown*: Sometimes, the options that come in front of us are things that we are not familiar with or aware of. There is a general fear of the unknown. In Ramya's case, her biggest fear was whether she'll be able to make it without a formal degree in marketing.
- *Early rejection*: When an individual tries to make a career shift, they are bound to get some early rejections. There may be people you connect with who will tell you that they don't consider career pivoters. They may only want people from a very specific domain and industry. They may seem like they are rejecting you. However, these may not even be the kind of organisations that will value your skills. Thus, it is important to know how you will manage these rejections.
- *Demotivation from others*: Our closest friends and family sometimes become our biggest demotivators. They don't do it out of malice but out of their own fear for us. Lochan has heard many clients say how their partner or family members are the first to ask if they will be able to survive in the new world. If we haven't done the first two steps, it will be very difficult to convince others of the real 'why' behind what we are doing.

- *Self-doubt*: Self-doubt will creep in. Almost everyone goes through phases of self-doubt. Whether you express it or not, you ask yourself if you will be able to make it. However, the extent and duration of this self-doubt can become a big deterrent in making this change.

While making the plan, also think of how to tackle these common pitfalls.

In the seven-step framework, Ramya overcame specific hurdles and mental blocks. These were:

- I don't have a degree in marketing. Can I build a career in it?
- I don't have great connections. Where do I start?
- How do I build connections? How do I use them for career transition?

We'll now look at some of these aspects in greater detail.

How to Build a Career in a Field Without Formal Education?

Can I do a job in which I do not hold a degree? Is formal education the only way to build a career? Let's find out.

If we asked you to visualise education, most of us would envision a classroom. The learners seek knowledge from one person in the room, known as the teacher. This concept of education originated in a religious setting. The disciples would sit around a priest or a scholar to learn from their deep knowledge of the world. This process worked well. Not everyone had the access or the means to do a deep study of the world themselves. Society relied on a few individuals to lead the way. Now that you think about the world today, this is actually a counter-productive way to learn.

Coming back to the original question—is formal education the only way to build a career?—the short answer is NO. Education is key to having a strong foundation for your professional life. But the definition of education is evolving. If you want to be a successful professional for a long time, you need to embody the following ethos:

- *Build a habit of learnability*: You should be ready to learn anything, anywhere and from anyone. Learning to learn is one of the highly rated skills desired by top employers. All organisations look for individuals who can learn new skills as they go. They view learning as a lifelong process, not a final destination.
- *Focus on the outcome and purpose rather than the content*: When you are in a classroom setting, ask yourself, 'Why am I learning this?' Then, try to visualise how you can use that knowledge in your life. When you focus on learning something new without understanding its use, you are more likely to remember it for a short time.

- *Focus on the practical implementation*: Learning without doing is like saying, 'I know all the swimming techniques. But I can't actually swim.' It's important to have a strong foundation. It's more important to understand how to use the knowledge. Hence, skills are more important than degrees as they showcase what you can do rather than what you know.
- *Be community-driven*: Yes, we all want lifelong friendships out of a college experience and we all deserve it too. But also look at your peers as a source of learning and try to build a community that drives you to be more. Peer-led learning is the best way to surround yourself with creative energies. It unlocks learnability and creates a network effect towards future work opportunities.

We are already seeing signs of the future.

- A 2024 survey by the Society for Human Resource Management (SHRM) found that 52 per cent of employers have relaxed their educational requirements to focus more on skills and experience.[1]
- A 2023 LinkedIn Workforce Report in the US revealed that 72 per cent of employers have dropped degree requirements for roles that previously required them.[2]
- New age start-ups are in the forefront of this movement. They make hiring bias-free and put skill first. This has

opened a new avenue of career progression for young talent. For example, over 50 per cent of India Inc. companies are now hiring via hackathons.[3]

Postgraduate programmes like Mesa School of Business and Masters Union emphasise hands-on work and experience rather than focusing only on classroom learning.

Studies show that there are various options available for learning and you can now own your learning journey, choosing the route that works best for you. You no longer need to rely only on formal courses or certification; you can choose the 'doing' path by volunteering and taking on side hustles, or take on part-time courses or programmes that let you learn the skills to put into a job.

How to Land Your Next Opportunity

There are several ways you can use to find out about new opportunities.

- The career portals of organisations are reliable sources of information about available job opportunities. Professionals can follow these pages to stay updated.
- LinkedIn pages of companies, specifically their job section, offer information on new opportunities.

- Companies often run job referral schemes for employees. Tapping into your LinkedIn network and getting referral from an industry colleague working in a different company can really make your case stronger for an available position.
- Sign up for different job portals that advertise opportunities regularly.

Early-stage and young start-ups are always looking for people for various job roles, often offering multidimensional roles and exposure. You can identify some such start-ups and reach out to someone in those companies.

Lochan, who runs a young start-up, shares some interesting insights. She says that while they keep hiring people, when you get 150+ applications for a particular role, it is very difficult to sift through all of that and find the best candidate. In addition, most applicants sound the same. On LinkedIn, for instance, there is a template that can be used to send DMs to the prospective employer for the job. When we post a role on our LinkedIn page, we get a lot of DMs, but about 90 per cent of them look identical. Here's an example:

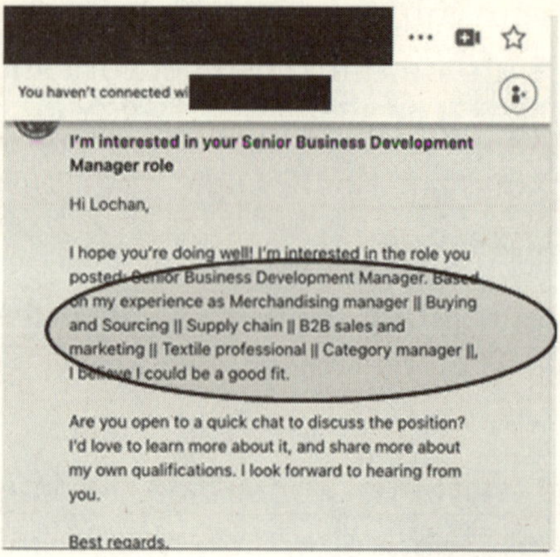

You haven't connected wi

I'm interested in your Senior Business Development Manager role

Hi Lochan,

I hope you're doing well! I'm interested in the role you posted: Senior Business Development Manager. Based on my experience as Merchandising manager || Buying and Sourcing || Supply chain || B2B sales and marketing || Textile professional || Category manager ||, I believe I could be a good fit.

Are you open to a quick chat to discuss the position? I'd love to learn more about it, and share more about my own qualifications. I look forward to hearing from you.

Best regards,

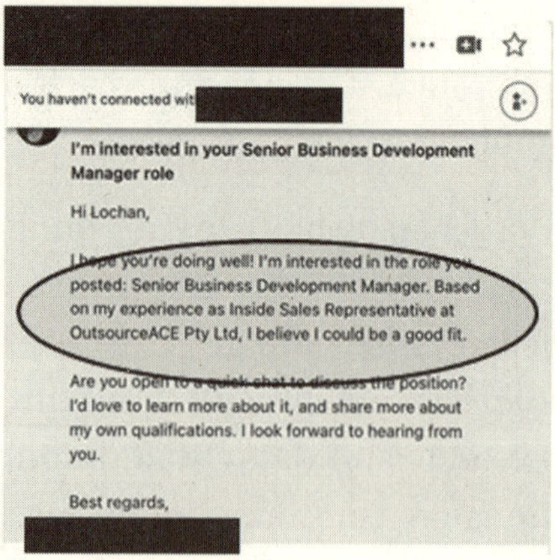

You haven't connected wit

I'm interested in your Senior Business Development Manager role

Hi Lochan,

I hope you're doing well! I'm interested in the role you posted: Senior Business Development Manager. Based on my experience as Inside Sales Representative at OutsourceACE Pty Ltd, I believe I could be a good fit.

Are you open to a quick chat to discuss the position? I'd love to learn more about it, and share more about my own qualifications. I look forward to hearing from you.

Best regards,

These are the pre-filled sections from your LinkedIn headline.

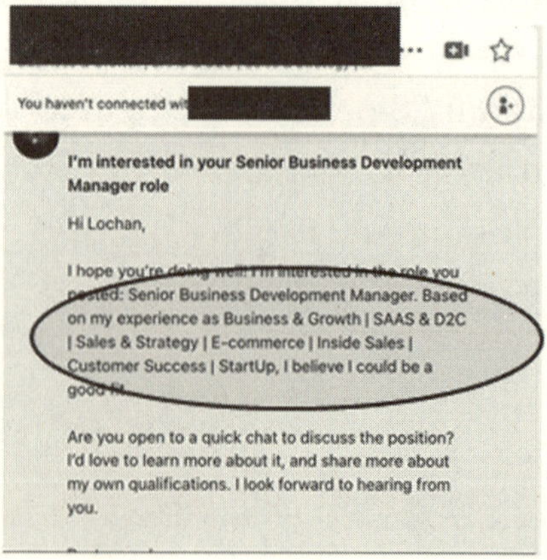

You haven't connected wi

I'm interested in your Senior Business Development Manager role

Hi Lochan,

I hope you're doing well! I'm interested in the role you posted: Senior Business Development Manager. Based on my experience as Business & Growth | SAAS & D2C | Sales & Strategy | E-commerce | Inside Sales | Customer Success | StartUp, I believe I could be a good fit.

Are you open to a quick chat to discuss the position? I'd love to learn more about it, and share more about my own qualifications. I look forward to hearing from you.

When there is no differentiation between any of the applicants, how will you stand out? And when we don't receive any response to our application, we often blame the recruiter, the company, our luck and so on. The fact is, we need to up our game when it comes to searching for and applying to relevant jobs.

Here are some mistakes you should avoid:

- *Spray and pray approach*: Sitting on any of the job portals all day and just clicking 'Apply' is called the 'Spray and Pray' approach. This means you are not selective about which organisations or roles you want to apply to. The 'Easy Apply' option of LinkedIn and other job portals makes it very easy for us to apply to jobs, but it also encourages us to just keep applying to any position or organisation that looks even remotely interesting (or even not!). It is not a surprise then that despite applying to a hundred companies, one barely gets shortlisted for any job.
- *A one-size-fits-all approach*: Professionals often create one resume and share it for all job opportunities. This doesn't work as company executives often spend only a few seconds to glance through your resume. Tailoring your resume as per job requirements is the key to moving towards the next steps. Application tracking systems (ATS) are tuned to look for certain keywords (from the JD) which need to be present in the resume for the system to shortlist a candidate. Thus, a single resume for different companies or roles will not land you anywhere.

- *Weak resume*: Many professionals make common mistakes in their resumes. These include misspelt words, missing contact information like phone numbers and emails, incomplete project details, and including too much irrelevant information.
- *Missing cover letter*: A lot of candidates skip the cover letter. But a cover letter gives you the space to make a strong first impression. Adopt a conversational tone and begin with a unique introduction. Research the company well before applying and build in some anecdotes into your letter that reflect what you'll bring to table. Convey why you think you are a good fit for the role.
- *Not utilising alumni connections*: Many professionals don't contact their college alumni. Alumni are a valuable resource for hidden job opportunities which are never advertised.
- *Missing social media profiles*: One of the first things companies do is to look at the candidate's social media profiles such as LinkedIn. Keep it updated and share the link in your resume.

How to Use Your Network to Land Your Next Opportunity?

How often do you wonder if your colleague's role would have been a perfect career move for you?

Many of us wait for our supervisors to suggest the next role for our career progression. However, the choices offered may not fit our career aspirations. For instance, if you want to move from IT delivery to a marketing role in your organisation, it would be unfair to expect your supervisor to help you make that move.

So how do you do it? The answer lies in the power of effectively leveraging your diverse network. As the famous saying goes: 'Your network is your net worth.'

What are some of the typical reasons you are not able to network?

- Lack of time
- Don't know how to do it
- Feel awkward

Research shows that networking can feel uncomfortable for many people, especially those who are shy or awkward.[4] It may take you longer to connect with others, or you might struggle with making a good impression. Perhaps you feel the need to compensate for your nervousness with false enthusiasm. Balancing the need to network with the desire to avoid discomfort can be a challenge.

Build up your networking skills by slowly getting out of your comfort zone. Take a small step by, say, talking to a colleague who works in the marketing department of your company. They can give you important information about the skills and qualifications you need, the tools and expertise required, current job openings and insights about decision-makers. The conversation will give you some confidence. You'll also come to appreciate the benefits of such an exchange. Building your network is a slow and steady process, but often the rewards of a diverse network are exponential.

Once you've started building your network, the next crucial phase is of nurturing it. Nurturing a network is like managing a piggy bank. If you haven't put any coins in it, you will only draw a blank. Coin refers to the value you have added to your network; you cannot always ask for value from your network without first giving value to your network.

For someone who is coming back from a career break, networking is even more critical. You need to start reconnecting with old colleagues, managers, acquaintances, etc. and establishing your network six to eight months before you actually start looking for a job.

Networking Mindset

The inability to network is less about logistics such as the availability of time, limited information or inaccessible opportunities and more about the mindset.

In her coaching conversations, Lochan often hears leaders tell her: 'Networking is an effort', 'I shouldn't have the need to network, my work should speak for me' and so on. But that's not how it works. The sooner we accept that networking plays a crucial role in our career and indeed in our lives, the quicker our path to progress will be.

If you want to leverage your networking skills before you start enrolling for networking events or reaching out to people on LinkedIn, here's how you can develop the right networking mindset:

- *Reframe your perspective on networking.* We often create stories in our minds about networking that can stop us from pursuing career opportunities. A common story people have is that they are introverted and hence are unable to talk to strangers at a networking event. But if we become aware of these stories, we can intentionally change them in a way that helps us.
- *Don't avoid networking because you are afraid people will think you're selfish.* Instead, consider what you can give. When you ask someone for career guidance or help, you give them a chance to contribute and add value. Many people appreciate this. There are many ways to add value creatively. One way to do this is by organising a virtual conference. Another way is by interviewing industry experts and sharing their insights. You can also add value by offering thoughtful feedback or new perspectives. By offering value first, you increase the likelihood that others will reciprocate.
- *Discover your genuine curiosity.* Many individuals love to discuss themselves. Before you meet someone new, research them. Approach it with genuine interest instead of trying to impress them by memorising the 'correct' questions to ask. This is a small shift in mindset, but it can have significant impact.

- *Highlighting your strengths and accepting your awkwardness can be beneficial during networking events.* In case you're not able to mask your unease, consider acknowledging it with humour. You can admit that you're feeling nervous or fidgety, or that you've forgotten someone's name; people will appreciate your genuineness.
- *Instead of putting on a façade, learn to accept your flaws and imperfections.* Be open and show vulnerability and humour. People value and appreciate these traits.

Networking is difficult for many people, especially for those who feel uncomfortable or shy in social situations. Despite the discomfort, networking is crucial for career growth and success. Many people make excuses or avoid networking. But there are tools that can help you overcome this challenge. One important step is to reflect on the stories you tell yourself about networking. Rewrite these stories in a way that feels authentic to you. Instead of seeing networking as one-sided, think of yourself as a giver in the interaction. Even if you have less power or connections than the person you're networking with, your unique perspectives and experiences can benefit them. Embrace your authentic self and recognise the value you bring. By doing this, you can build meaningful relationships that support your career growth.

Let's explore the steps that can help you leverage networking for career transitions.

Networking for Career Transitions

If you want to make a career transition, how will you know about new opportunities or avenues if you don't connect with people outside your immediate circle? Networking is relevant not only from a perspective of 'landing a job' but even for 'gathering relevant information' about that job. As you set out to network with a career transition in mind, remember three things.

1. Be precise and have an elevator pitch

When networking for career transitions, be clear about what you want. Instead of asking vague questions like 'Can I pick your brain?' or 'Let me know if you can help?', be specific. For instance, if you want to connect with an innovation lead at a tech company, ask if anyone knows someone in that role. This approach helps others understand how they can help you.

When introducing yourself at a networking event, don't state your job title. Instead, communicate the benefits of what you do. For instance, instead of saying 'I'm an IT project manager', say 'I help my banking client by ensuring their website provides a smooth experience, delighting millions of customers.'

Networking and sending helpful emails to people you admire is an important practice. It is a good habit to develop, and you should not expect anything in return. Increasing your 'luck surface area' can also enhance your career prospects. To succeed, focus on creating new opportunities, building your brand and meeting new people. When asking for help or favours, offer something in return. Asking without giving anything first is called taking value and can limit your success. The best networkers give something valuable before asking for anything in return.

Your elevator pitch is a concise presentation of yourself typically conveyed in thirty to sixty seconds. It mainly covers:

1. What makes you unique
2. What you are seeking
3. What you can offer
4. What you want a person to remember about you.

In short, your goal is to focus on the essential and say who you are, what you do and what you want to achieve.

2. Use platforms like LinkedIn for internal and external connect

Build luck into your career!

To be successful in your career, you need some luck. But you can increase your chances by actively embracing serendipity. One way to do this is through serendipitous networking. Instead of just trying to get something out of others, connect with them to learn from their experiences and perspectives. You can discover valuable insights and get inspired to grow in your career by asking thoughtful questions and listening carefully. To succeed in your career, it is important to be open to change and see it as a chance to grow. The COVID-19 pandemic has shown us how much our lives can change, and it has also shown us that there are new opportunities for jobs and careers. Some people have been able to make the most of these changes by following their interests and learning new things.

LinkedIn enables you to connect with professionals in your industry, former colleagues, classmates and potential mentors or mentees. You're no longer limited to your immediate colleagues within office premises. Some of these connections can lead to new career opportunities or guidance.

Over the last few years, Gaurav grew his LinkedIn network from a few hundred connections to more than twenty-five thousand. Here are some tips that worked for him:

- Start with low-hanging fruits: Add colleagues (past and present) and college and school mates.
- Time it well: After attending an event, send a LinkedIn invite request with a brief personal note.

- Expand and strengthen your current network: Reach out to people who are relevant to you and share common connections.

However, before you start sending connect requests to random people, there are two things you need to be mindful of. First, how does your LinkedIn profile look?

Does your profile look like this?

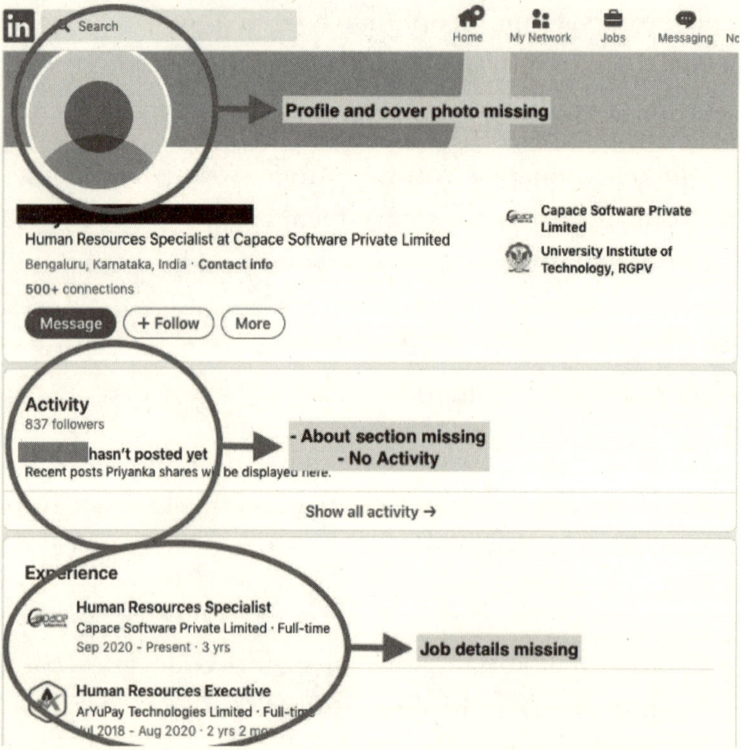

If so, then the first step is to work on your profile. Invest time in sharing information about yourself which is useful for others. In today's times, LinkedIn is a digital CV that speaks a lot about what an individual does and where their interests lie.

Recruiters often search for people on LinkedIn. If your profile doesn't have the right words that recruiters are searching for, you might miss out on a big opportunity.

Second, how to connect with people on LinkedIn?

As you write to people, whether it is to add them to your network or to apply for a role, try and build a genuine connection. They don't know you, so start by introducing yourself: tell them who you are, where you got to know about them, why you find their profile interesting and your reason for connecting with them. The reason could be anything—information, industry insights or expertise, advice and mentoring, and so on.

People, more so those who have made successful careers for themselves, receive a lot of LinkedIn connects and DMs and don't reply to quite a lot of them. The reason is the messages are often impersonal and lacking in information about the purpose.

If you don't explain why you want to connect with someone, it is difficult for the other person to make time for you. So make sure your DMs are not like the ones shown below:

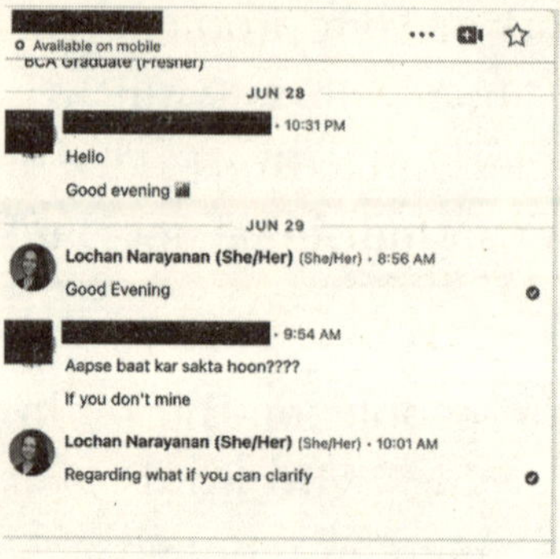

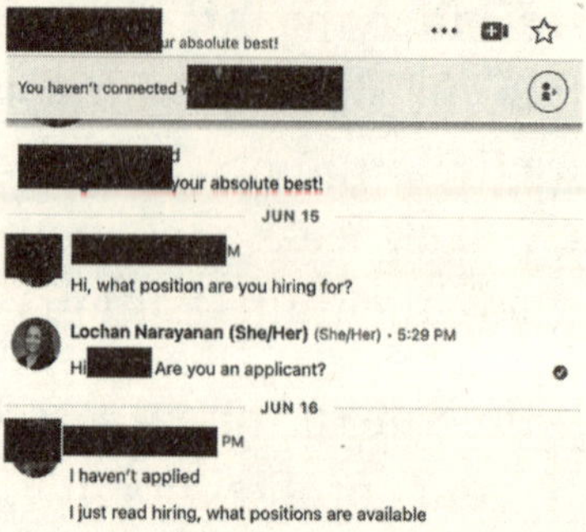

Instead, write like this:

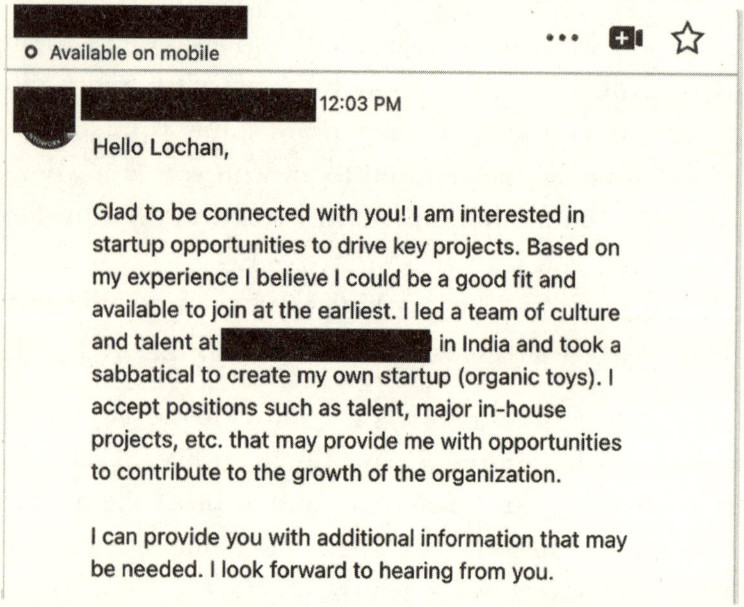

The idea is to provide information and present a context to the other person, to elicit a response from them. People will be happy to invest time if they understand why and who they are investing their time in.

3. Create a strong personal brand

Nahia Orduña's article 'How to Build Your Personal Brand at Work' shares important insights on personal branding.[5] She says: 'Building a personal brand is a real investment and can be tricky when you're giving yourself fully to your job. It's even more difficult for young professionals, who may have less experience to build from. So, how do you get started? The trick is to make your personal brand a fulfilling part of your day-to-day job.'

Orduña suggests that you can describe your personal brand by determining three key factors:

1. *Your distinctiveness*: What fresh or uncommon point of view do you offer to the company?
2. *Your principles*: What drives your work or what do you believe in?
3. *Your contributions*: Based on your professional background or education, what skills can you offer to your industry?

These three factors combine to create your unique personal brand.

Showcase your work by creating and sharing content. If you don't have content that highlights your efforts, people won't know what you have achieved or what you believe in. Take an hour or two at the end of your day or week, or whenever works best for you, to create content. Start by reposting news or articles that align with your personal brand on social media platforms.

We think of social media influencers when we hear the term 'personal brands'. They show their talents by singing, dancing, modelling or talking about fashion and fitness. These individuals are renowned for their knowledge and are aware of the latest trends. They are considered trustworthy by their followers. Now, imagine if you could achieve the same level of impact in your workplace. Consider the advantages to your career if people in your industry seek your guidance and motivation. Building personal brands has become increasingly popular among employees, and with good reason. Staying current with industry trends helps you adapt and be resilient. Being recognised for your qualities and abilities improves your visibility, access to opportunities and professional advancement. Building a favourable personal brand benefits you and your organisation. But why don't more people develop their personal brands? In our opinion, it's because they lack time. Building a personal brand requires commitment, which can be difficult given the demands of modern-day jobs. This is even more challenging for young professionals with less experience. But no matter how difficult it may be—and it will be difficult when you're just starting on this journey of building your personal brand—you must do it. Think about what you are known for—or what you'd like to be known for at work.

Here are some tips to get you started:

Step 1: Develop your personal brand

When you work for corporations, it's easy to get caught up in their culture and lose your own identity. Gaurav says, 'I have always been proud of my employers, wearing their colours and using their language. If you are like me, how can you create a personal brand that co-exists with the larger corporate identity?'

To do this, you must identify three factors:

- *Your uniqueness*: Think about the many aspects of who you are: your background, culture, race, ethnicity, gender, sexual orientation, class, caste and religious beliefs. How does your identity influence your understanding of the world and the business? What unique perspective do you bring to the organisation that nobody else can? Remember, your differences are your strengths.
- *Your values*: What do you stand for? What global, domestic or community-level issues are you passionate about? Look at UN Global Issues or PWC reports to find inspiration. Climate change, equality, health, human rights, sustainability and disruption are some causes that may drive your actions or give you a sense of purpose at work.
- *Your contributions*: With your business experience or studies, what can you bring to the table in your

industry? If you have a background in psychology, your understanding of human behaviour can help you offer valuable feedback to the marketing team. Perhaps you are a UX designer who can create more accessible products. Or you may be talented in analytics, telling data-driven stories about business strategies. Whatever your expertise, how can you use it to add value to your work, team or industry?

The combination of these three elements creates your personal brand.

Take the example of Gaurav, who is passionate about industry–academia partnerships, with an international background, and has experience working in the domain of IT, HR and innovation (uniqueness). He is also a gold-certified mentor and workplace-certified coach and wants to help people from diverse backgrounds find the right jobs and make relevant career transitions (values). In his last role he worked at a group innovation centre for a big company. People come to him for career advice on getting into innovation. His professional and personal identity combine to create a unique personal brand. This brand represents him, his values and his expertise.

If you don't consider yourself an expert yet, don't worry. Building a professional personal brand is a journey that requires learning and time. Even if you lack the necessary skills, you have something valuable to contribute. You should determine what you can offer at present and commit to developing that area of expertise, knowing that it's okay if it evolves.

Step 2: Look for initiatives and goals that match your brand

After determining the focus of your brand, it is crucial to find ways to apply it in your everyday work. You should include it in your professional development goals and make it a regular part of your tasks. Review the projects your team is currently working on and determine if any of them align with your brand. If they do, express your interest in participating. If not, explore further and examine what is happening at the organisational level. Major corporations publish yearly reports on topics such as sustainability, DEI (diversity, equity and inclusion) and workforce development. Read through them and engage with teams working on issues that interest you.

Step 3: Connect with colleagues who have similar interests

To be successful, incorporate your personal brand into your work. Collaborate with colleagues who share your interests. Colleagues can inspire, support, criticise constructively and give fresh perspectives. They can also help you improve your ideas. For instance, if your brand wants to make the workplace more inclusive for first-generation employees, find colleagues who can assist you with this goal and give you feedback. You can start by joining employee resource groups (ERGs) that create safe spaces for different identities. You can also take the initiative to share articles or videos you're passionate about with your team members.

Step 4: Create and share content

Creating and sharing content is a crucial part of building your personal brand. Your content can showcase your abilities and values, even if your projects or work change. Make sure to include your own perspective. As you practise, you will feel more at ease expressing your thoughts in writing. You might even start creating your own content, such as opinion pieces, social media posts or videos. Keep in mind that producing original content requires more time and effort. If your content is thoughtful, ethical, well-researched and unique, people will appreciate it and engage with it. Expect feedback, both positive and critical, and use it to improve your future content. As you become more visible, you may have chances to speak at internal or external events, which will need you to create new content. You can use iterations of that work to develop new ideas to publish or post.

Sita's story is amazing. It shows how she developed her personal brand and made successful career transitions. Sita comes from a lower-middle–class family where it was difficult for her parents to even pay her school fees. She got her master's in astronomy and space physics. She couldn't do her Ph.D. because she didn't have enough guidance and support.

Eventually, she did a computer course at NIIT and got a job at a small company as a software developer. She had the chance to learn and perform different roles in a small organisation. She did marketing, sales and customer demos. She also learnt how to do these roles, which helped her grow faster. During this time, she continued to interview for better opportunities. She gave around a hundred and fifty interviews but didn't succeed in any of them. However, she didn't give up. She learnt from her failures and eventually got a job at a medium-sized IT services company. After some experience she went for an interview for one of the big IT services companies and got selected. Her career trajectory changed when she received guidance and mentorship from an excellent mentor. Interacting with her mentor helped her recognise her own worth. As a result, she quickly rose to become the lead and achieved the first award of her life. After four years she moved to IBM practice and worked there for ten years. She fondly recalls how every year she along with her team would focus on one IBM product and take it to newer heights within her organisation. She focused on one priority every year. This included upskilling herself and her team with certifications, focusing on analyst relations, participating in IBM awards, and representing customer advisory boards. Eventually, this led her to be promoted as global lead for emerging technologies in 2019. She also joined Women in Technology (WIT) and the NASSCOM panel for AI & Technology. This enhanced her brand value and established her as a leader in the emerging technology field. She shared her networking secrets. She maintained her network by connecting with trainees joining the organisation and helping account managers with customer proposals. Building a wide network had a multiplier effect. Senior people would take on leadership roles within or outside the organisation, and junior people could potentially join her team in the future. She also reviews her career every six months to reflect on what she can do to break any pattern of monotony that may be emerging in her worklife.

Sita strongly believes that mentors play a crucial role in shaping one's career. She quotes one of her mentors, who was a senior HR leader: 'Understand your worth and demand it.' Sita considers herself lucky to have had senior leaders as mentors from outside her organisation. They have encouraged her to take a strategic and top-level perspective on things. She remembers her life mantra fondly: 'I trained my mind to always do my best, no matter how small the task.' Learning something new or taking on a new role can be challenging. Many of us think it's very different from what we were trained in. As a result, we often do it without much enthusiasm. This leads to underperforming and feeling frustrated. Thus, it is important to keep our learnability hat on at all times.

Key Takeaways

- Create an action plan to make a career transition.
- You can build a career even in a field where you lack formal education.
- Use your online presence to land your next opportunity.
- Be patient and do not leave a role within a few months of joining.
- Develop your EQ. Having relationships with people in your industry can be one of the best ways to land a new job. It can also help you get valuable insights and stay informed about deals or opportunities you wouldn't find out about otherwise.
- Make a connection. Point people to useful resources. And keep an eye out for opportunities you can give to others. It always comes back around. Ten times over.

chapter seven

Will You Never Feel Stuck Again?

SAMEENA, A CIVIL ENGINEER WHO GRADUATED FROM Mumbai University, began her career with an EPC company that designed and built plants for the chemical and oil industry. She worked there for six years. Then, she joined a global energy company as a structural engineer. Over time, she advanced to a prestigious role as an auditor in the corporate function. In this role, she travelled to different company offices worldwide and interacted with the leadership team. She again moved to an unconventional role and became an underground engineer based on her mentor's advice. This turned out to be a great learning ground for her and paved the way for her next promotion as a section head. After a few years of working in this field, she changed her track and moved to a very prestigious role as an internal auditor.

The world of work has evolved, and professionals are open to making multiple switches based on what's right for them at that point in time.

Do Roles Have an Expiry Date or Do We Just Keep Evolving?

You can always outgrow a role. Today, the world is moving at a fast speed, and skills that keep you relevant in the professional environment are constantly evolving. This could be a bane or a boon, depending on how you look at it. Those who believe in acquiring one skill early in life and then building a career around it might struggle moving forward. Those who can constantly learn would be able to stay relevant but will also find themselves outgrowing roles in their current organisations.

How do you figure out that you have outgrown your current role? After speaking to group of professionals who have gone through such a career path, we have compiled a list of signs that might help you answer that question:

- Your daily tasks come too easy or do not challenge you at all.
- You are constantly getting excited about other roles/ jobs available out there.
- You have stopped learning on the job—there is no upskilling needed to perform your role.
- You don't see any signs of progress or evolution in your current role.
- You have the feeling of being undervalued in your current set-up.

What should you do when you find yourself at such a crossroads? This book is something you can keep coming back to as your compass in navigating this amazing adventure of a career. You can start doing all the exercises again from Chapter 1. Find what's right for you, how you can make the next move and build an action plan. Our endeavour is that it will enable your journey at different crossroads and motivate you to take that leap of faith. Finally, we hope the book will also serve as a reminder that there have been many before you and there will be many more after you on a similar journey. At the moment, it might feel like you are alone and taking a big risk but we are here to remind you that it has been done and can be done!

The Future of Being a Professional

Moving forward, you don't have to lock yourself in one role. You can explore diverse areas of passion. You can hold a full-time job in accounting while exploring data science on weekends. You can also lead a sales team while upskilling yourself in organisational development. You can switch roles based on your interests. This will allow you to branch out as you grow in your professional journey. It will help you meet your potential. As society evolves, the lines between a professional and a freelancer will also blur. It will become a norm for some to hold two to three full-time leadership roles. It could also mean that you might be a CTO in the morning and a bar owner by evening. Besides multipotentiality, another major trend will disrupt careers for the next couple of decades. It is generative AI. In the last twelve months, graduating students have often asked Apoorv, 'Do I need to be afraid of ChatGPT as I build my career?' Apoorv feels if he could charge a hundred rupees every time someone asks him that question, he would be rich enough to at least afford flying business class domestically!

Early stage funded start-ups need a lot of strategic thinking and are always on the lookout for multipotentialites. They need support and domain expertise. Yet, the founders are usually cash strapped and don't have the necessary expertise or time. They can't hire senior leaders to do this. Thus enters a 'fractional CXO'. They provide the required expertise but are not committed to the company for the entire time. They agree on time or output commitment. This gives the senior individual flexibility. They can explore different industries and still 'own' their time. Their payment can be a combination of retainership, success fee and stock/equity options. The concept of fractional/partial CXO is taking over. This is especially true for roles like CHRO, CFO and CTO.

New-age companies have made this possible by being open to having part-time leaders. This gives them the flexibility to afford someone out of their budget. Another reason for this trend is the newfound trust in remote work. People focus more on results than on time spent working. Finally, individuals are no longer leaving their growth in the hands of one company. Instead, they give their personal development and self-actualisation more importance. The ecosystem enables this shift.

We had a detailed conversation with Anubhav, a new business sales leader for Cloudflare in Canada, who has changed his job multiple times. He previously held similar roles at SalesForce, Shopify and CarDekho. He has been part of five different organisations over the last seven years. His longest stint at any organisation lasted three years. He has worked in India and Canada. So, not only has Anubhav moved jobs and industries, he has even moved countries for work. He still managed to build a beautiful career for himself. The course he studied or the knowledge he gained during his higher education did not relate to any of the roles he has had so far. I find this fact to be the most interesting aspect of his journey. It's interesting to observe how he perceives the evolution of a professional. It's intriguing to see how he believes you actually build it, step by step. Let's look at an excerpt of the conversation.

> *Is formal education the only way to build a career? Or even the right way? How much of what you learnt in the classroom helped you at the job?*
>
> No and maybe. Hardly anything I learnt in college has helped in my job. However, stuff that I learnt in and more importantly, the way I learnt in high school has been very useful in my job(s).
>
> *What is the future of being a professional? Do you believe it would still be one job for a fixed duration of*

time or multiple roles at various places or something else?

I imagine you mean one job for a fixed time (independent contractor) vs multiple roles at various places at the same time (gigs). From the data I've seen, both ways of working are growing. And I believe in the former more than the latter. I think professionals will be coming together more freely, and I still believe you should have one primary 'job' that you dedicate your focus to.

How did you pivot and how often? You have moved around roles, sectors. How easy/difficult was it for you? Any recommendations?

I pivoted because I didn't like something about my current situation—environment/people/money come to mind. Change is never easy but sometimes it's necessary. So my advice is to always be conscious of WHY CHANGE, WHEN do you want to CHANGE, WHAT CHANGE do you want, and then get started on HOW. Things that have worked for me, and what I'd recommend:

- Get CLEAR about the WHY/WHEN/WHAT. You need to be able to articulate it in a way that makes sense to you and to others.
- Talk to people who have been directionally successful in what you're trying to do.
- Take their ideas and start experimenting.

How do you build a career in a world where skills eat knowledge? Or do they?

Skills don't eat knowledge. Skills are informed by knowledge. Someone with hundred units of knowledge exercising 10 per cent of those as skills will likely build a better career than fifty units exercised at 10 per cent. My usual method is to ask:

1. What are you trying to achieve in your career? What 'things' do you need to do in order to achieve what you want? Where is the gap?
2. Then expose yourself to new ways (new to you) of doing those 'gap things'.
3. Understand how those new ways may be better suited to achieve the outcomes you want vs the ways you already know and exercise.
4. Try them out. Let the rubber hit the road.
5. Reflect on what went right and what could be better.
6. Rinse and repeat.

Do we do everything or one thing or nothing at all? Are we moving away from the world of specialists? What is your take and experience?

We do everything that we can do with focus and presence. You have to look at your life as a balance of health, work and relationships. A third of your waking hours are dedicated to each, maybe not every day but through the course of a week/month/quarter/year it should be relatively evenly spread out.

We always are moving away from old world specialists, to a newer set of specialists with the pace of change increasing. (It's how the universe works, accelerating always.) At a human lifetime scale, you will always need to be a solid generalist but then have a spike of specialisation depending on your inherent talents/inclinations/market demand.

We have had many conversations like these with people who have been on their early–mid-career journey. They anticipate exploring the unknown instead of settling for the 'good known'. This makes us believe that these days roles do come with an expiration date. It might differ based on industry, but you can't escape it. Yes, there will always be outliers. Most organisations now plan for an employee to stay with them for two to three years in junior roles. They also expect employees in middle management to stay for five to seven years. This trend and data should be liberating for you if you are starting your career. You don't have to put too much pressure on yourself to find the perfect internship or first job. Instead, ask yourself these three questions:

1. Will I learn from this experience?

2. Does the sector or the role spark some sort of interest or enthusiasm in me?
3. Does it cover my basic financial need at this stage of life?

If you focus on the now and try to enjoy each experience in the present rather than overmapping it to your ten-year plan or some grand retirement scheme, you might find it all anyhow.

Lastly, why did we choose to call this book *Career Heist*. From our respective lived experiences, we have realised that now more than ever you need to take charge of your professional journey. Things are not constant anymore; we are in the middle of the most rapid technological evolution witnessed by humankind.

It's in the benefit of an organisation to have you do the same role over a long period of time as that brings in continuity and stability. But the same can make you feel imprisoned as a professional. And when you do feel imprisoned, it's time for you to design your own Career Heist! Hope the tools, stories and our experiences presented in this book help you construct your heist with minimal damage to any stakeholders attached and most importantly help you push forward in your journey.

Key Takeaways

- You can outgrow a role with time.
- You can explore diverse areas of passion. You can hold a full-time job in accounting while exploring data science on weekends. You can also lead a sales team while upskilling yourself in organisational development. You can switch roles based on your interests.
- When you feel at a crossroads again, you can return to this book and redo all the exercises to navigate this amazing caeer adventure.

Acknowledgements

IT WAS A STORMY WEATHER AND A DELAYED FLIGHT THAT brought the three authors together and gave birth to this crazy idea of co-authoring a book on careers. However, this idea would have just been left on the pages of our *'little black book'* without seeing the light of the day, if it wasn't for the unconditional support of the below folks. They were the first ones who believed in us and in the concept and displayed their confidence in us by fully backing us on this project.

Thank you so much for your unwavering support and we hope we did you proud through this work.

Abhishek Mawai	Bharat Parashar	Nikhil Chopra	Sandhya Chebiyyam
Aditya Bose	Chaithali Prasad	Nikhil Deshpande	Sanjog Wadhwani
Ajay Sanghani	Chinmaya Dave	Nisarg Shrivats	Sannika Kalra
Akhilesh Sharma	Deepak Sanchety	Pallavi Nagarkar	Saugato Bhowmik
Alfana Khatri	Dilip Bhapkar	Poonam Anil	Saurabh Nagesh

Alok Pradhan	Dipti Janardhana	Pranav Chaturvedi	Shantanu Chakraborty
Amit Mediratta	Divya Janardhana	Prasanth Nambiar	Shazia Hakim
Amol Mujumdar	Faisal Ansari	Praveer Singh	Sheetal Sharma
Anand Vinekar	Fayyaz Khan	Preeti Ogale	Shivprakash Swami
Anant Tyagi	Gurpreet Kalra	Prerna Agarwal	Shreyash Parihar
Anjana Nair	Hita Hejmadi	Priyanka Naik	Shruti Arora
Antony Vivek Prasanna	Ishita Ray	Prosenjit Aich	Shruti Jaiswal
Anubhav Razdan	Kamal Chandran	Raj Rani Bhalla	Suman Katarki
Arijit Sarkar	Kiran Aatre	Rashmi Verma	Sushant Kadam
Arjun Patnaik	Kokila Roy	Ravi Karthik	Swaminathan Ramesh
Arjun Siva	Manish tiwari	Roli Pandit	Sweta Surana Bhandari
Arun Bhardwaj	Milind Maheshwari	Roma Divanji	Umang Vanjara
Arun Surana	Mohit Chhabra	Sakthi Vinodhini M	Vedashree N
Arvind Balan	Munish Markan	Samir Ekbote	Vidushi Malhotra
Atreya Roy	Nida Zahara	Sandeep Jain	Vinay Tripathi
			Yogendra Singh

Endnotes

Chapter One: Are you feeling stuck?

1 Bart Turczynski, 'Biggest Career Regrets Revealed: Learn from Others' Mistakes', 9 July 2024, https://zety.com/blog/biggest-career-regrets.

2 Michelle Gibbings, 'How to Build a Career You Won't Hate', Harvard Business Review, 8 February 2022, https://hbr.org/2022/02/how-to-build-a-career-you-wont-hate.

3 Mark Chussil, 'Why You Should Approach Your Career Like a Game', *Harvard Business Review,* 14 September 2021, https://hbr.org/2021/09/why-you-should-approach-your-career-like-a-game.

4 Calvin Rosser's tweet dated 9 April 2021, https://x.com/calvin_rosser/status/1380314150983725061.

5 John Coleman, '6 Signs It's Time to Leave Your Job', *Harvard Business Review,* 8 February 2022, https://hbr.org/2022/02/6-signs-its-time-to-leave-your-job.

6 Read more on these steps in Akash Khurana, *Mentormorphosis: Stories for Mentoring the Leader in You* (Rupa Publications, 2022).

Chapter Two: Is It Too Late to Change Your Career?

1 Rajiv Gupta, 'Next-gen Technology Disruptors', *Mint,* 28 December 2022, https://www.livemint.com/companies/people/nextgen-technology-disruptors-11672243539732.html.

2 Manu Balachandran, 'How Technology Has Changed the Way We Live, Work and Socialise', *Forbes India*, 10 May 2019, https://www.forbesindia.com/article/10th-anniversary-special/disruptions-of-the-last-decade/53457/1.

3 Guneev Puri, 'Prompt Engineering in India- Scope, Demand and Courses', Naukri Blog, 27 September 2023, https://www.naukri.com/blog/prompt-engineering-in-india-scope-demand-and/#.

4 Jeroen Kraaijenbrink, 'What BANI Really Means (And How It Corrects Your World View)', *Forbes*, https://www.forbes.com/sites/jeroenkraaijenbrink/2022/06/22/what-bani-really-means-and-how-it-corrects-your-world-view/.

5 India Life Expectancy, 1950–2024, https://www.macrotrends.net/global-metrics/countries/IND/india/life-expectancy.

Chapter Four: Finding What's Right for You

1 Nicholas Pearce, 'Why Purpose—Not Passion—Should Guide Young Professionals', *Harvard Business Review*, 25 October, 2019, https://hbr.org/2019/10/why-purpose-not-passion-should-guide-young-professionals.

2 Lauren C. Howe, Jon M. Jachimowicz and Jochen I. Menges, 'Your Job Doesn't Have to Be Your Passion', *Harvard Business Review*, 4 June 2021, https://hbr.org/2021/06/your-job-doesnt have-to-be-your-passion.

Chapter Five: How Do You Land Your Dream Job Without Quitting?

1 Ryan Roslansky, 'LinkedIn CEO Ryan Roslansky: 'Your Next Best Employee Is Most Likely Your Current Employee', *Fortune*, 20 March 2023, https://fortune.com/2023/03/20/linkedin-ceo-ryan-roslansky-best-employee-careers-leadership-tech/.

2 Shivani Shinde, 'IT Industry Logged 25% Attrition in FY22, Trend to Continue: Report', *Business Standard*, 29 September 2022, https://www.business-standard.com/article/economy-policy/it-industry-logged-25-attrition-in-fy22-trend-to-continue-report-122092900620_1.html.

Chapter Six: How to Make Your Next Move?

1 Ajit Soren, 'Skills Based Hiring Trends & Statistics for 2024', *WeCP*, 30 May 2024, https://www.wecreateproblems.com/blog/skills-based-hiring-trends-statistics.

2 Dan Schwabel, 'The Shift Away from College Degrees in Employment', *LinkedIn*, 16 January 2024, https://www.linkedin.com/pulse/shift-away-from-college-degrees-employment-dan-schawbel-wnoge.

3 TechGig Bureau, '50% India Inc. Companies Participate in Hackathons for Focussed Hiring', TechGig, 13 May 2022, https://cio.techgig.com/research/50-india-inc-companies-participate-in-hackathons-for-focussed-hiring/articleshow_b2b/90954675.cms.

4 Alyssa F. Westring, 'The Awkward Person's Guide to Networking', *Harvard Business Review*, 20 September 2021, https://hbr.org/2021/09/the-awkward-persons-guide-to-networking.

5 Nahia Orduña, 'How to Build Your Personal Brand at Work', *Harvard Business Review*, 28 September 2022, https://hbr.org/2022/09/how-to-build-your-personal-brand-at-work.